Legendary **Brides**

Legendary **Brides**

LETITIA BALDRIGE

A HarperCollins*Publishers*/Madison Press Book

FIRST EDITION

Library of Congress Cataloging-in-Publication Data on file

ISBN 0-06-019559-2

00 01 02 03 04   10 9 8 7 6 5 4 3 2 1

Produced by
Madison Press Books
40 Madison Avenue
Toronto, Ontario
Canada M5R 2S1

Printed and bound in Italy

*It is my hope that
brides-to-be, their mothers,
and friends will find
inspiration and magic
in these intimate portrayals
of celebrated brides.
Memorable weddings begin
with cherished traditions
and heartfelt vows.
May this book be your
guide to the most beautiful
moment of your life.*

— Letitia Baldrige

CONTENTS

INTRODUCTION

A WEDDING IS a wondrous event. No pageantry unfolds with more drama, and no one remains unaffected by witnessing the celebration. It is, after all, one of the most beautiful moments in a woman's life. The guests assembled to take part in the ritual are aware that a new family is beginning. It is a solemn, moving occasion. Or should be.

Today's bridal couples no longer feel the pressure to marry as their grandparents did. In fact, they often take great pains to avoid doing so, going as far as getting married in a fire watchtower high above the pine trees of a national park, or jumping from a plane with their pastor — a trio of colorful parachutes having a ceremony aloft for the benefit of the wedding guests watching below.

Traditionally, brides have consulted their mothers in the matter of what kind of wedding to have. Mother decided, father paid, and bride complied. (The groom usually had no say whatsoever.) The great old families still have traditional weddings because they "can't let the family down." Great-uncle Harold's portrait would fall off the mahogany-paneled wall if his great-niece were to sully the family name with an inferior, informal, or even wacky wedding.

Now that we have entered a new millennium, old and young alike are hungry for beauty, tradition, and old-fashioned values. *Legendary Brides* is, therefore, a salute to the year 2000, with some of the great weddings of the nineteenth and twentieth centuries serving as inspiration for the brides of today. The weddings of most of the "legendary brides" in this book had enormous influence on the fashions and entertaining styles of their day. Today's brides, for example, owe a great deal to Queen Victoria, whose wedding to Prince Albert of Saxe-Coburg and Gotha on February 10, 1840, was the talk of the world. Before Queen Victoria, a bride simply wore her best dress, whatever its color, for a brief ceremony in church. But the Queen's white satin and lace-trimmed gown, her lace veil held by an orange-blossom wreath, and her twelve bridesmaids in pastel dresses set the fashion in weddings for years to come.

I have been privileged to know some of the legendary brides of our time, one of them the most celebrated of her day. I was a nineteen-year-old student in Paris when I had the great good

(Above) In a moment from another legendary nineteenth-century wedding, Princess Alexandra's lovely bridesmaids — eight in number — prepare for her marriage to the Prince of Wales in 1863.

fortune to meet the elderly, but still beautiful and regal, Consuelo Vanderbilt in her Paris home. She was the most prominent in a wave of turn-of-the-century American "dollar princesses" who married into European aristocracy, bringing with them money and New World vitality in exchange for the social currency of a titled husband.

Consuelo's wedding to the Duke of Marlborough in 1895 attracted worldwide coverage and generated huge public interest. (After reading in the newspaper that her garters had gold clasps studded with diamonds, Consuelo wrote, "I wondered how I should live down such vulgarities.") The marriage, arranged by Consuelo's mother, was more noteworthy for the splendor of the ceremony and the wedding breakfast that followed than for the wedded bliss of husband and wife. Knowing the Duke had married her only for her money, Consuelo divorced him after eleven difficult years and found real happiness in her marriage to Jacques Balsan and in working for women's causes. I will never forget her long, swanlike neck, set off with exquisite dog collars of pearls and diamonds, and her thick, long hair, which she still wore upswept.

This is mostly a book about first-time brides, but we have made one important exception. How could we not, when the most eligible man in the world, Edward VIII, gave up his throne to wed a twice-divorced woman from Baltimore in a 1937 ceremony that riveted the world. Wallis Warfield Simpson, famous for her flawless taste, chose a romantic French castle — the Château de Candé — as the setting for their wedding. The rooms were filled with the extravagant scent of lilies and white peonies, and the bride appropriately did not wear white, but a pale blue crepe satin dress by her favorite designer, Mainbocher.

I remember my mother's remark when she saw the Windsors on the Movietone News.

"It's plain to see," she said triumphantly, "that the Duchess has her own personal maid. Otherwise, she could never get in or out of that dress for all the tiny buttons on it."

When my old school friend Jacqueline Bouvier married Senator John F. Kennedy in the summer of 1953, I was hard at work in Rome for Ambassador Clare Boothe Luce. In those days, there was no jetting across the Atlantic for special occasions, so I missed the wedding of the year. It was remarkable not only for the magnificence of the bride's dress; it was unique because of the striking looks and remarkable promise of both the bride and groom. This

I was so proud of you and thrilled at having you so close

to me on our long walk in Westminster Abbey, but when I handed your hand to

the Archbishop, I felt I had lost something very precious. . . .

— George VI, writing to his daughter
Princess Elizabeth after her wedding

match "promised fairy tales for the future," one writer noted. On September 12, more than seven hundred guests crowded into St. Mary's Church in Newport, Rhode Island, to watch the handsome couple exchange vows. After the Archbishop of Boston read a special blessing from the Pope, the bride and groom were whisked away to an outdoor reception at Hammersmith Farm, the country estate of Jackie's mother and stepfather. The crush of reporters and photographers outside the church made it almost impossible for the wedding party to leave, but "Papa" Joe Kennedy's goal of maximum publicity for his politically ambitious son had been achieved.

I never could have guessed then that only eight years later, Jacqueline Kennedy would be America's First Lady and I would be working in the White House as social secretary. In May of 1961, we planned a special luncheon for the Prince and Princess of Monaco. Once America's movie princess, Grace Kelly had given up her act-

ing career for a royal title, marrying Prince Rainier of Monaco in an extravagant state wedding on April 19, 1956. Her father remarked that the ceremony was "a grand production. I felt I was in Hollywood watching them shoot a Cecil B. DeMille film." Hundreds of cameras brought the image of a luminous Grace, resplendent in over three hundred yards of Valenciennes lace, to magazine covers all over the world. In fact, the young couple would have much preferred a quiet wedding. At the end of a week of festivities, they were totally exhausted — a perfect example of a wedding that became so elaborate that its most important participants could not enjoy it as much as they would have liked.

The media's interest in Grace Kelly's wedding paled in comparison with the frenzy displayed during the wedding of the twentieth century's most famous princess. But despite the modern demands for pictures and publicity, the 1981 wedding of Lady Diana Spencer to

Prince Charles was steeped in tradition. In addition to the setting in St. Paul's Cathedral and the solemn ritual of the marriage service, the bride's attire and her bouquet held many connections to the past. Diana wore the Spencer family tiara and a pair of "borrowed" diamond earrings from her mother. Antique lace that had once belonged to Queen Mary was worked into the panels of her dress, and the myrtle in her bouquet had been picked from bushes grown from cuttings taken from Queen Victoria's wedding bouquet.

angel, and said, "I don't care. My dress is just as pretty as hers, my wedding was just as beautiful, and my guy, let's face it, is a lot more handsome than that prince!"

Today's brides should not feel that tradition has no part to play in their ceremonies. Carrying a great-grandmother's prayer book, wearing a grandmother's necklace, or working a mother's favorite flower into the bouquet are every bit as "traditional" as wearing a family tiara.

Every detail of Diana's wedding signaled a return to a romantic age. One look at the sweeping folds of her spectacular ivory silk taffeta gown and women everywhere wanted to emulate her. Brides of that era wanted an equally extravagant look, but in perfect taste. It wasn't until Carolyn Bessette's 1996 wedding to John F. Kennedy Jr. — in an understated and utterly stunning pearl-colored silk crepe slip dress — that brides embraced the sleek and unadorned style that still continues to influence wedding gown design today.

When looking at the spectacular weddings of the brides in these pages, I am reminded that money, beauty, and celebrity do not necessarily equal happiness. I remember attending a small wedding in a midwestern church, with a fruit punch reception held afterward in the church parlor. Everyone was talking about the recent wedding of Princess Diana and Prince Charles. The bride linked her arm with mine, looked up at me with the smile of an

Consuelo, Wallis, Jackie, Grace, and Diana are but a few of the legendary brides described within the pages of this unique book. It is my hope that brides-to-be, their mothers, and friends will find inspiration and magic in these intimate portrayals of celebrated brides — borrowing ideas for flowers from this wedding, a cake from that one, a bridal-gown flourish here, a reception idea there. The splendor of a royal or society wedding may be beyond most budgets, but bringing a sense of style, ceremony, and tradition to a wedding is far more important than the amount of money spent — and that is something every bride has the ability to do. It just takes a little imagination and the willingness to learn from the triumphs and disasters of the famous brides who have gone up the aisle before her.

Letitia Baldrige

CHAPTER ONE

THE ROMANCE
OF VICTORIA'S WEDDING

Really, I do not think it possible for any one in the world to be happier, or as

happy as I am. He is an Angel, and his kindness and affection for me is really touching....

What I can do to make him happy will be my greatest delight.

— Queen Victoria's journal,
February 11, 1840

QUEEN VICTORIA'S marriage to Prince Albert of Saxe-Coburg and Gotha on February 10, 1840, set the stage for the beautiful, romantic weddings we hold today. Although it is hard to imagine the dour, black-gowned Queen Victoria as a lovestruck young bride, when she was twenty, the tiny British monarch became a wedding trendsetter.

Unlike many royal marriages of the time, Victoria and Albert's was a love match. After they were introduced in 1836, Victoria wrote in her journal, "Albert . . . is extremely handsome; his hair is about the same colour as mine; his eyes are large and blue, and he has a beautiful nose and a very sweet mouth with fine teeth; but the charm of his countenance is his expression . . . full of goodness and sweetness, and very clever and intelligent." She proposed to him on October 15, 1839. "It was a nervous thing to do, but Prince Albert could not possibly have proposed to the Queen of England. He would never have presumed to take such a liberty."

The date of her proposal remained forever special to Victoria, and she had it engraved in Albert's wedding band. Although the Prince had given Victoria a diamond friendship ring four years before their marriage, her engagement ring would be considered decidedly unusual today. It featured a snake with diamond eyes! In the nineteenth century, snakes were popular emblems of love, their wound coils symbolizing eternity.

The headstrong young monarch oversaw all of the wedding preparations. She was the first royal bride to ignore the tradition of wearing a heavy brocade dress decorated with jewels and half hidden by a velvet-and-ermine mantle. Instead, she ordered a lovely white satin gown trimmed with sprays of delicate orange blossom. Although white silk or satin dresses had been *de rigueur* for "best dresses" since the 1820s, Victoria's choice of one for her wedding made them popular bridal gowns as well.

In one area, Victoria did not ignore tradition. Her gown, like other bridal dresses of the era, was trimmed with lace. Lacemaking is an ancient feminine art, even older than the weaving of cloth. In the sixteenth century, lengths of bobbin lace, made by crossing and twisting thread around pins on a small pillow, were used to trim bridal posies, much as a length of lace ribbon is used today. Later, the manufacture of needlepoint lace, which was made with tiny stitches overlaying larger stitches on a paper pattern, supported

(Opposite) Queen Victoria's wedding dress of rich white satin, trimmed with sprays of delicate orange blossom and yards of handmade Honiton lace, revolutionized bridal gown design and set the romantic style for white dresses that is still followed by brides today.

many communities throughout Europe. Generations of lacemakers laboriously produced the same secret patterns, their precious fabric named for the towns in which they lived: Alençon, Lyons, Chantilly, Honiton. By Victoria's time, machine-made lace was available, but wealthy brides or those whose ancestors had spent many hours producing family heirlooms still wore hand-crafted lace.

Jane Bidney, a lacemaker from Beer, outside Honiton, was commissioned to supply the handmade lace for Victoria's royal dress and fingertip-length veil. Jane, who had never been outside Devon, fainted from nerves while waiting to be received by the Queen in London. Once she recovered, the two women discussed the lace for the neck and sleeve frills and for the front panel of the wedding dress. It took more than one hundred lacemakers six months to make the exquisite lace. (The average time for making 1½ square inches of lace is from five to eight hours.) In appreciation, Victoria invited Jane to attend the ceremony and sent each of the lacemakers £10 to celebrate the wedding.

On February 10, the Queen awoke to a steady downpour. Shortly before nine she wrote a charming note to Albert, who was staying at the palace:

> Dearest — How are you to-day,
> and have you slept well? I have rested very well and feel very
> comfortable to-day. What weather! I believe,
> however, the rain will cease. Send one word when you,
> my most dearly loved bridegroom, will be ready.
> Thy ever-faithful, Victoria R.

This small message of concern for her husband-to-be, who had suffered from seasickness on a stormy five-hour crossing of the English Channel, shows not only Victoria's thoughtfulness but also her passion and her anticipation of what her life together with Albert would be like.

After breakfast, her governess gave Victoria a "dear little ring" while she was helping her former pupil with her hair and wreath of orange blossoms. The Victorians loved accessorizing — with lockets, cameos, long drop earrings, and jeweled hairpins and combs — and their queen was no exception. Diamonds glittered in Victoria's hair, a diamond necklace graced her neck, and Prince Albert's gift of a sapphire-and-diamond brooch sparkled over her heart, the traditional spot for a brooch on an English bride's wedding day.

While Victoria was getting ready at Buckingham Palace, the wedding guests filed into the Chapel Royal of St. James's Palace, and the twelve young bridesmaids gathered excitedly in a room set aside for the Queen and her attendants. In contrast to the extravagant gowns and jewels of the women guests, the bridesmaids were a study in understated loveliness. Their enchanting white tulle dresses, trimmed with creamy white roses, had been designed by the bride herself in the classic ballerina style that continues to inspire wedding gown designers today.

About noon, Prince Albert's carriage left Buckingham Palace, followed a short while later by Victoria, her mother, and her Mistress of the Robes in the royal coach — as thousands lined London's Mall, waving and cheering. In the century ahead, Victoria's children, grandchildren, and great-grandchildren would follow the same route on their wedding day.

One of the bridesmaids, Lady Wilhelmina Stanhope, remembered Victoria's arrival at St. James's: "The Queen was perfectly composed and quiet, but unusually pale. . . . I thought she trembled a little as she entered the chapel, where Prince Albert, the Queen Dowager, and all the Royal Family were waiting for her." The bridesmaids picked up her train and followed her up the aisle as the national anthem played. Victoria appeared to recover at the sight of Albert and throughout the ceremony gazed into his eyes, tears welling up in her own as he said the words, "With all my worldly goods I thee endow."

Victoria's was the first royal marriage ceremony to be held during the day. More than five hundred guests packed the floor and gallery of the Chapel Royal in St. James's Palace to witness the young monarch exchange wedding vows with her beloved Albert.

At the end of the ceremony, to great applause, the royal couple walked arm-in-arm to the Throne Room, where they and their families signed the registry book. Victoria then gave each of her bridesmaids a gold brooch, inlaid with diamonds, rubies, and pearls, in the shape of the eagle on her new husband's crest. Gold rings were also presented to honored guests. The Queen handed out six dozen, each one engraved with her profile and the inscription "Victoria Regina." Victoria had a natural gift for public relations and understood the lasting value of these ceremonial gifts — the rings were treasured by the recipients, proudly shown all over the Empire and handed down as great family treasures.

A wedding "breakfast," which featured an immense cake weighing three hundred pounds, was held at Buckingham Palace for a small group of family and friends. Victoria then changed into a white silk dress trimmed with swansdown and a white velvet bonnet. "Dearest Albert came up and fetched me downstairs, where we took leave of Mamma and drove off at near 4, Albert and I alone which was *so delightful*."

The young Queen's obvious love for her new husband and her fairy-tale wedding — with its romantic flourishes of diamonds, lace, and white blossoms — touched the hearts of women throughout the world and influenced bridal style for generations to come.

WITH THIS RING, I THEE WED

I felt so happy when the ring was

put on, and by Albert.

— Queen Victoria's journal,
February 10, 1840

ALTHOUGH DIAMOND engagement rings became accessible to a larger population only after the discovery of diamond mines in South Africa in 1870, the practice of the groom giving the bride a gem-set ring had been firmly established many years before. Symbolism played an important part in the design of these early rings. Rubies for love, diamonds for loyalty, the bride's or groom's birthstone — all were considered appropriate for the engagement ring. But the wedding band, a symbol of endless love, was never decorated because it was considered bad luck to break the circle with a gemstone.

In Shakespearean times, many women were given gimmel, or twin, engagement rings, which featured two interlocking hoops. When the hoops were slid together, they gave the impression of a single ring. What could be more symbolic! Secret messages of love engraved inside could be read only when the ring was separated. Two other romantic symbols — the heart, and two clasped hands —

appeared on seventeenth-century rings and remained popular into the Victorian era. Sometimes the two hands were incorporated into a gimmel ring that, when pulled apart, revealed a tiny heart.

Early in the twentieth century, platinum guard rings set with colored gemstones were worn by married women who wanted a flash of color on their ring finger. The guard ring was slipped on behind the diamond engagement ring. More recently, an elaborate gold wedding ring has sometimes taken the place of an engagement ring. A diamond is often set in the center of the wide gold band or smaller stones are worked into a patterned design. It is placed on the bride's finger by the groom at the traditional point in the wedding ceremony and is not seen in public until then.

The romantic designs of the past are proving popular with a new generation of brides, and antique rings are now enjoying a revival. Exquisite, one-of-a-kind rings and bands can be found at

ANNOUNCING YOUR ENGAGEMENT

❧ Promoting family harmony is obviously important at this exciting time. Call your prospective in-laws to tell them you're engaged and how lucky you feel to be marrying their son. If your fiancé's parents are divorced, call each one, and stepparents, too.

❧ New beginnings should be taken advantage of enthusiastically. It does not matter if one or both people who become engaged have been married before. I don't recommend e-mailing your news to family members and good friends. Such exciting news should be conveyed directly by telephone or in person.

❧ If a small, intimate wedding is planned, both the bride's and the groom's sides should mention this as they are spreading the happy news. This will help avoid hurt feelings later, when invitations to the wedding are not received by some friends or relatives.

CHOOSING THE PERFECT RING

*T*HE FIRST STEP in finding the perfect ring is dealing with a reputable jeweler, one who comes well recommended and belongs to a national jewelry industry association. The store should be able to provide a large selection of diamond or precious-stone styles in every price range and in a variety of settings — yellow gold, white gold, platinum, or a combination two-tone look. Buying the wedding band at the same time as the engagement ring is a good idea.

Diamonds are classified according to what diamond merchants call the four Cs: cut, color, clarity, and carat.

CUT

❧ Not to be confused with the shape or outline of a diamond, the cut refers to the arrangement and proportion of a diamond's facets or planes. How well a diamond is cut determines its sparkle and fire. Brilliant-cut stones have fifty-eight facets that reflect light, while step-cut stones have fewer facets and thus less brilliance.

COLOR

❧ Diamonds are rated on a color scale from D to Z. At the upper end of the scale (D to F), the stones are colorless, and at the lower end (S to Z), they are light yellow. The less color in a diamond, the more valuable it is — although brown, blue, pink, and yellow diamonds are expensive because of their rarity.

CLARITY

❧ Very few diamonds are flawless. Fortunately, with the exception of step-cut stones, imperfections in stones rated SI2 or above are not visible to the naked eye. The fewer the flaws, the more valuable the diamond.

CARAT

❧ Diamonds are weighed in carats, which are divided into points (one carat equals 100 points). Larger stones are less common, thus more expensive. However, the value of a stone cannot be determined by carat weight alone.

Some couples want new, one-of-a-kind rings. Queen Elizabeth's engagement ring, for example, was designed for her using diamonds that had originally been part of a tiara belonging to Prince Philip's mother. Master jewelers and designers can make rings using their own custom designs or one provided by the bride and groom. Antique rings — either a relative's or something seen in a magazine — can be copied, too.

After you have chosen your rings, be sure to get a certificate from your national gemological institute and a written appraisal of the replacement value of the rings for insurance purposes. List the rings separately on your personal property insurance, or if you are still living at home, list them on your parents' policy until after the wedding.

A double-ring ceremony symbolizes the exchange of marriage vows between a man and a woman. If the groom has chosen to wear a wedding band, it is usually the same color of metal as the bride's. It does not need to be the same design, but if it is, his ring is often a few millimeters wider. The bride is responsible for ordering her fiancé's ring and having it engraved.

reputable antique shops and auction houses — and often cost less than comparable new rings. A word of caution: since a gemological certificate cannot be given, it is advisable to have the jewelry appraised. You should also ask the jeweler to check that the stones are not loose.

Engraving the inside of wedding rings is an ancient practice. A Greek betrothal ring from 400 B.C. carries the single word "Honey." In the sixteenth and seventeenth centuries, rings bearing short poems or "posies," some of them quite whimsical — "Love him who gave thee this ring of gold, Fore he must kiss thee when thou art old" — were popular expressions of affection. Victorian rings were sometimes engraved with a series of seemingly meaningless letters. When examined closely, however, the letters spell the interlocked names of the young couple, one name reading to the right, the other to the left.

Today many couples have their wedding bands engraved with both sets of initials and the wedding date. Some follow the old practice of adding a personal inscription. And most honor the ancient tradition of wearing the ring on the fourth finger of the left hand — from where, romantic legend tells us, a vein runs directly to the heart.

Round Brilliant

Pear

Oval

Marquise

Emerald

Heart

DIAMOND SHAPES

The shape of diamond you choose for your engagement ring is largely a matter of personal taste. In general, round-shaped diamonds look flattering on women with small hands and short fingers. Square-shaped diamonds suit a woman with longer fingers. Most diamonds are cut into one of six classic shapes.

❧ ROUND BRILLIANT. This is the most popular shape for engagement rings and the best "sparkler," since this cut transmits more light than any other. Very small brilliants, called "single cuts," are sometimes used as side stones in rings. Prince Edward and Sophie Rhys-Jones chose an engagement ring featuring a large, central round brilliant flanked by two heart-shaped diamonds.

❧ PEAR. One of Elizabeth Taylor's most famous jewels was the Taylor-Burton diamond, a 69.42-carat pear-shaped stone given to her by Richard Burton.

❧ OVAL. This shape reflects light almost as dramatically as the round brilliant but appears larger than a brilliant of the same carat weight.

❧ MARQUISE. Widely chosen today because of the popularity of solitaire rings, the marquise is named after Louis XV's mistress, the Marquise de Pompadour, who preferred her gems cut in this shape. The extra labor involved in cutting the diamond makes it more expensive than a round brilliant of a similar size and quality.

❧ EMERALD. Named for the stone that is often fashioned this way, the emerald cut has less sparkle than a round brilliant but is a very elegant look nonetheless. A variation is the princess cut, which is square rather than rectangular. Princess Grace of Monaco's engagement ring was a 12-carat emerald-cut diamond solitaire.

❧ HEART. This was the romantic choice of Victorian poets Elizabeth Barrett and Robert Browning.

MAGICAL GOWNS

I wore a white satin gown

with a very deep flounce of Honiton lace,

imitation of old.

— Queen Victoria's journal,
February 10, 1840

JUST AS VICTORIA chose lace for her wedding dress that was "imitation of old," brides today can find inspiration in the past. Over the years since Victoria's wedding, dress designers have come up with every imaginable style of gown — from the simplest of sheaths to extravagant ball gowns fit for a princess. The most beautiful ones are those made with true craftsmanship and exquisite fabrics. These dreamlike confections complement the bride rather than taking the spotlight away from her. To feel breathtakingly beautiful, comfortable, and, above all, true to one's own personality and sense of style is what every bride wants on her special day.

After Victoria's wedding, brides followed the young Queen's lead. Instead of marrying in a new "best dress" of a fashionable color, they chose a beautiful white gown — setting in motion the tradition of the white wedding dress, which has continued to this day. The Victorian bridal dress, with its form-fitting bodice and full skirt and train, remains a classic as well. By the late 1860s, the crinoline had been replaced by the bustle, which remained popular for the next twenty years. Toward the end of Victoria's reign, bustles had disappeared and fashion's emphasis shifted to the top of the dress, which featured billowing leg-o'-mutton sleeves and a very elaborate bodice topped by a high wedding-band collar of boned chiffon and lace. The look of both Victorian and Edwardian brides was modest, graceful and feminine. It is perhaps best summed up by a writer in a 1905 issue of *The Ladies' Home Journal*: "A white muslin gown with a tulle veil, a few flowers at her belt and in her hair — she will look like some sweet white flower."

After the First World War, bridal wear reflected the changing role of women. Corsets were thrown away, hair was cut short, and "high-spirited" rather than "dainty" became the fashion watchword. The famous French designer Coco Chanel showed the first short wedding dress. Although the new bridal frocks fell just below the knees, they were still white and still embellished with frills, ruffles, and pretty decorations. The glamorous Hollywood bridal look of the thirties, with its slim sheaths and shimmering fabrics, gave way to Victorian-style full skirts and scoop necklines in the fifties, a reflection of the traditional roles women resumed after the Second World War. During the free-spirited sixties and seventies, many brides rebelled against tradition by wearing outfits that ranged from minis and caftans to funky hippie gowns. It was not until 1981, when Lady Diana Spencer's elaborate taffeta gown captured the imagination of the world, that formal bridal attire once again became the height of fashion, ushering in a decade of extravagant designs.

As we enter a new century of bridal style, a bride can draw on a hundred years of evolving fashion to choose exactly how she wants to look on her wedding day — sweet, romantic, modern, traditional, full-skirted, slim-sheathed, or daringly low and definitely sexy! And if she chooses well, her bridal gown will reflect both the romance of the occasion and her own personality.

(Opposite) An ethereal wedding gown of shimmering silk organza by designer Romona Keveza combines the romance of the past with a clean, contemporary silhouette — featuring illusion sleeves that echo the slender shape of calla lilies, and a chapel-length veil strewn with tiny seed pearls.

DRESS DETAILS

FABRIC

The choice of dress fabric depends on both the location of your wedding and the season in which it takes place. Floaty, filmy fabrics, such as chiffon, georgette, organza, linen, and silk crepe, are ideal for spring and summer or for a wedding held in a tropical climate. Fall and winter weddings that take place in northern climates call for heavier fabrics, such as brocade, velvet, and wool crepe. Satin, taffeta, and tulle are appropriate year-round.

Lace still adds its exquisite touch to wedding gowns. Reproductions of ancient patterns are made by machine today — with the exception of Queen Victoria's pattern, which was destroyed so that it could never be copied. Old lace can also be used to trim a newly created gown. This is a wonderful way to incorporate the lace from your mother's or grandmother's wedding dress or veil into your own design. A reputable bridal salon will be able to guide you in selecting the best style to achieve this custom look. Old lace can be found in vintage clothing stores and antique shops.

COLOR

Ivory, rather than true white, was considered the best color for wedding dresses in Queen Victoria's day. Today's bride can choose from a range of whites — from the brightest white to delicate cream and the palest ivory. Dresses in a light hue of gold or silver are now also popular, as are dresses with just a hint of pink or soft blue. Wedding consultants recommend trying on gowns in several shades to see which one is best suited to your skin tone.

A blush satin rose adorns the lace sleeve of a romantic period wedding gown.

TRAINS

Flowing trains are guaranteed to make a bride feel regal. Unlike Victoria's, though, trains today tend to be shorter. Often they are detachable — fastened at the waist during the ceremony and removed afterward — or "bustled," using a system of hooks or snaps. Choosing the appropriate length of train is determined by the formality and location of the ceremony, the style of your gown, and your height.

❧ SWEEP. This most subtle of trains is actually the back of the gown's skirt that brushes the floor. The style is suitable for a garden wedding or a semiformal wedding. It is also appropriate for a formal wedding when worn with a chapel-length veil.

❧ CHAPEL. The chapel train, which extends about one yard, is the most popular choice for a formal wedding.

❧ CATHEDRAL. This train extends farther than one yard and is reserved for very formal weddings. The most recent royal brides — Mathilde d'Udekem d'Acoz of Belgium, Sophie Rhys-Jones of England, and Princess Alexandra of Greece — wore gowns with cathedral trains.

❧ COURT. The court train features a flat piece of fabric that falls from the shoulder or just below the shoulder blades. The length of the train may be sweep, chapel, or cathedral. The wedding gown of Elizabeth, Victoria's great-granddaughter, featured a court train.

❧ WATTEAU. Like the court train, the watteau cascades from the shoulders or just below the shoulder blades. However, this train is always pleated or gathered. It is usually chapel or cathedral length.

DETAIL WORK

I am a long-standing member of the "less is more" school. When a bride adds glittery jewelry to an overly embellished gown, she begins to look like a walking chandelier. However, well-chosen details — a delicate line of embroidery, a touch of lace, or a simple pattern of seed pearls or beading — can make a dress truly special. Although Victorian wedding dresses were overly ornate by today's standards, the details they employed provide lovely touches for today's dresses — be it a tasteful accent of handmade silk flowers on the bodice, a perfect row of buttons marching down the back of the gown, or an inset of lace. The contemporary design below, made of Italian silk satin, was inspired by Queen Victoria's sumptuous wedding gown.

CLASSIC BRIDAL GOWN STYLES

The choice of style for a wedding gown should be based on the type and size of wedding planned (an outdoor wedding in the country does not require the formality of a big wedding in a city cathedral or synagogue), the season and climate, and the bride's figure type. A clinging slip dress may not be the best choice for a full-figured bride, while a ball gown may look fabulous. An A-line dress with vertical seams looks wonderful on most brides, and an empire style will make a petite bride look taller. Although you should always keep your budget in mind, purchase the best style you can afford. Remember, you will be immortalized in your dress through your wedding photographs. There are five basic dress silhouettes from which to choose.

This classic princess silhouette features a box-pleated skirt trimmed with French Alençon lace.

❧ A-LINE. The fitted bodice and A-line-shaped skirt of this style flatter almost every figure type. The classic version — the princess style — features vertical seams that create the gown's shape.

❧ EMPIRE. The empire silhouette has a high waistline placed just below the bust and a straight or A-line skirt. This style creates the illusion of height and often makes the waist look smaller.

❧ SHEATH. This narrow silhouette with its long, lean lines has a number of variations ranging from form-fitted to semi-fitted. A woman with a slim, well-toned figure looks beautiful in a form-fitted sheath, while a woman with a fuller figure may find a semi-fitted sheath more becoming.

❧ BALL GOWN. This gown features a fitted bodice and a full skirt. The waistline of the bodice may be natural, dropped, or basque (dips in a V at the front of the dress). Princess Grace and Jacqueline Kennedy both wore ball gowns. A ball gown is particularly flattering on a bride who has a small waist and full hips.

❧ SLIP. The slip dress features spaghetti straps and a soft, flowing shape. It emphasizes a beautiful bosom and, depending on the way the dress is cut, can be flattering on various figure types. Carolyn Bessette wore a bias-cut silk crepe slip dress at her wedding, and completed her sleek look with long white silk gloves and a simple veil of hand-rolled silk tulle.

Ball Gown

(Left) A timeless silhouette, this strapless ball gown of silk satin features a drop waist and fitted bodice. The tulip-paneled back highlights the sumptuous chapel-length full skirt, which is accented with handmade satin flowers and a perfect row of tiny covered buttons that trails from the bodice to the hem.

A-Line

(Above) A square neckline and pleated cummerbund enhance the clean lines of this classic A-line dress. The Italian silk satin bodice flows into a romantic tulle skirt.

Slip Dress

(Right) This delicate slip dress of silk chiffon embroidered with seed pearls features a scoop neck and soft watteau train.

Gowns by Romona Keveza

Sheath

(Left) This classic semi-fitted sheath
of silk Dupioni, lavishly embroidered with seed
pearls, features a batteau neckline and a
loosely fitted silhouette that enhances the
figure of almost every bride.

Empire

(Above) From the royal courts of Europe
comes the inspiration for an exquisite empire
gown that includes a watteau train and a
strapless bodice encrusted with seed pearls
and tiny beads of Austrian crystal.

Train

(Right) Folded like intricate origami,
a detachable court train transforms
a simple A-line dress of silk satin
into a dramatic work of art.

Gowns by Romona Keveza

IN THE FITTING ROOM

A BRIDE IS SELDOM alone in choosing her gown. Suddenly, her mother, sisters, future sisters-in-law, and her twenty-eight "best friends" become her advisers. In fact, just about anyone aware of her upcoming wedding is seized with a desire to offer unsolicited advice. Your life will be much more serene if you enlist the services of a reputable bridal salon with the expertise to help you achieve the look you want. In fact, a full-service salon can be both a pleasant and a satisfying one-stop shopping experience. The majority offer a large selection of gowns to suit most budgets, as well as the accessories needed to complete your look — shoes, headpieces, and veils.

Keep in mind that bridal salons usually operate by appointment, so call ahead before you visit. And make sure the company you choose is well known and comes highly recommended. Take your wedding planner with you — with your clippings of wedding dresses, veils, and hairstyles — and show the consultant your favorite gowns. Remember, in spite of the fashions seen in many Hollywood weddings, this is the time in your life to look regal and beautiful. If you are being married in a religious service, a measure of modesty is not only proper, it is necessary.

A bride-to-be can make her bridal consultant's job easier in several ways. Bringing along a strapless bra and a pair of shoes with the heel height that will be worn at the ceremony is useful. Wearing a hairstyle similiar to the one planned for the wedding gives a better idea of what a headpiece or veil will look like with a gown. And graciously accepting help when trying on fragile dresses keeps them in immaculate condition.

As you start trying on various styles of gowns, remember that most bridal salons carry only one dress per style — and the size may not be the one you need. Here again, the help of an experienced bridal consultant is invaluable. She can guide you in choosing the most flattering style for your wedding day.

Once a gown is chosen, it will be ordered in the proper size. You should ask for a written agreement covering the dress specifications, the dates for the fittings, the delivery date, a cost breakdown (including alterations), and the method of payment. Be prepared to place your order well in advance of your wedding date — the average delivery time can be six months or more — and to place a 50 percent deposit on your gown. After being measured, some brides make the mistake of ordering a gown in a smaller size because they think they will lose weight before the ceremony. Remember that it is easier to take in a dress than to let it out. Generally, two appointments are made for alterations — one close to the delivery date of the gown, and the second a few weeks before the wedding — although more may be necessary to ensure an exact fit.

Consultants can provide advice on the undergarments that should be worn with the gown to make it look its best — a strapless bra? a petticoat? a full-length slip? a padded bra? Once you know what to buy, splurge on the best-fitting undergarments you can afford. And don't forget to bring these with you to your first fitting.

After your dress is zipped, buttoned, or slipped on, it is important to walk around the room. Here are some questions to ask yourself in the fitting room. Is the dress comfortable? Can I reach up to throw my bouquet? Can I bend down to listen to my flower girl? Will I be able to dance in it? It is excruciating to watch a woman on her wedding day in a badly fitted or too-tight dress.

According to experts, after you bring your wedding dress home, it should be removed from its plastic bag, hung on a padded hanger, and covered with a white cotton sheet. Attach a checklist to the top of the hanger listing all the items you will need to assemble on your wedding day, from the inside out — undergarments, panty hose, shoes, jewelry, and keepsakes.

Whether your dress is a romantic ball gown or a sleek sheath, a full-service bridal salon will make sure it fits well — and that you look your loveliest on your wedding day.

TRADITIONAL ACCESSORIES

I wore my Turkish diamond necklace and earrings, and Albert's beautiful sapphire brooch.

— Queen Victoria's journal,
February 10, 1840

WEDDING TRADITIONS link us to our past — to the brides in our families who have come before, each with her own hopes for the future. One tradition that has found its way from England to Victoria's former colonies is the charming rhyme:

Something old, something new,
Something borrowed, and something blue;
And a silver sixpence in your shoe.

Most of today's brides dispense with the last line, but the first two are still followed in many families and have been for generations. The "something old" — an heirloom veil or a piece of jewelry, for example — is provided by the mother of the bride or a married sister and is said to pass on the good luck of her marriage to the new bride. In the same vein, "something borrowed" can come from a happily married friend, who is passing on her happiness. The "something new" is often represented by the wedding dress. "Something blue" can be traced to the brides of ancient Israel, who wore blue to symbolize fidelity and love, and to early Christian brides who wore blue to symbolize the purity of the Virgin Mary. A touch of blue can be found in a garter, a piece of jewelry, or the bouquet.

Lovely old family traditions — a cherished strand of pearls, a family prayer book, an heirloom dress or

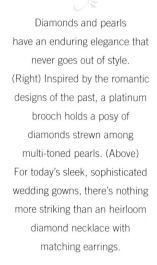

Diamonds and pearls have an enduring elegance that never goes out of style. (Right) Inspired by the romantic designs of the past, a platinum brooch holds a posy of diamonds strewn among multi-toned pearls. (Above) For today's sleek, sophisticated wedding gowns, there's nothing more striking than an heirloom diamond necklace with matching earrings.

veil — honor brides of the past and are sweetly nostalgic for the bride's mother and grand-mother. Even a grandparents' bride-and-groom cake topper can be passed on or reproduced.

There is no reason, of course, that a couple cannot start a new family tradition or include heirlooms from a previous generation. A handmade lace ribbon for the bridal bouquet could be made from an old piece of family lace; a beautiful brooch could serve as a sparkling hair ornament; a diamond bracelet could be just the right touch for today's sleeveless dresses.

A diamond bracelet — often a gift from the groom — has graced the wrist of many legendary brides, including Jacqueline Kennedy.

THE TIMELESS APPEAL OF FANS

Fans were very popular as engagement or wedding gifts from the 1700s through the Victorian era. During the reign of George II, they were sent to relatives and friends by the bride-to-be to announce her engagement. These fans were copies of the engagement fan given to her by her fiancé.

Today, fans can add a pretty, old-fashioned touch to a modern wedding. An antique fan is a particularly suitable accessory for a Victorian-style wedding dress, although lace ones tend to yellow over time and only work well with an off-white or cream dress. At outdoor summer weddings, fans can serve a practical purpose as well. Guests at the wedding of Vice President Al Gore's daughter, Karenna, to Andrew Schiff were given white fans decorated with the couple's names to help ward off the Washington heat, and as a delightful memento of the occasion.

This dazzling fan, with its elaborate baroque design, was carried by Princess Stephanie of Belgium when she wed Prince Rudolph, heir to the Austro-Hungarian Imperial Crown, on May 10, 1881.

KEEPING A WEDDING PLANNER OR JOURNAL

A wedding planner contains all of the information and logistical details necessary for the planning of a wedding. In addition to checklists and charts, it should also provide enough room to include: photographs and drawings of bridal gowns; ideas for bridesmaids' dresses, with color and fabric swatches; photographs of bouquets, boutonnieres, and floral arrangements for the ceremony and reception; pictures of accessories (shoes, gloves, handbags, hair ornaments); photographs of hairstyles and veils; music selections for the ceremony and reception; names of musicians and singers; photographs of sites for the ceremony and/or reception; and pictures of wedding cakes.

Preparing for a wedding can be a time when emotions run the gamut from bliss to despair. Some brides-to-be have found it useful to keep a wedding journal or to write their thoughts in their planner.

Journal writing can help with problem solving, sorting out emotions, and focusing one's thoughts. And even a simple recounting of events can be delightful to read in later years and can become a precious keepsake to pass on to children and grandchildren.

To serve as inspiration, here are two journal excerpts, one from the past and one from the present.
The first one was written by Princess Marie von Thurn und Taxis, who was married in Venice in 1875:

I can still picture myself coming out of my room in my wedding-dress (the incurable frivolity of the daughters of Eve prompts me to remark that it looked charming when it arrived from Laferrière's). Mamma had pinned on my veil of point d'Angleterre, the same she herself had worn at her wedding. Poor Thérèse was shedding tears all the time. Anette, Felicitas, my nice Tuscan maid Lina, my dear Antoinette who had come all the way from Fribourg — they all surrounded me and each of them wanted to assist in adorning the bride.

The second is a sample entry from one of my daughter-in-law's friends, written three nights before her wedding:

Nothing is ready. Absolutely nothing. The mini-tiara being constructed out of Mom's jewelry to hold my veil — the bridal salon says they can't work with Mom's diamond and pearl bracelets like they said they could. Mom is hysterical. I would be, too, if it weren't so much like a comedy special. My little sister offered the necklaces from her Barbie doll collection. At this point, I couldn't care less about the tiara. Forget it. Attach the blooming veil to my head with Velcro, for all I care!

Something Borrowed

English royal brides include a sprig of myrtle in their bouquets, picked from
the same shrub that supplied the greenery for Queen Victoria's bouquet. You can begin a similar
tradition in your own family by including ivy, another symbol of wedded bliss.

Wearing lace on one's wedding day is a tradition that dates from Victoria's time.
Lace ribbon is also a beautiful alternative to satin ribbon for bridal posies. If handmade,
it becomes a family heirloom to be tied carefully on future bouquets.

Victoria's lacemakers were grateful for her token of appreciation for a job well done.
Thank-you notes or small gifts to people who helped you with your wedding are thoughtful gestures.

Like Victoria's note to Albert on their wedding day, a note left
for your fiancé to find on your wedding morning is a romantic start to your life together.

Instead of engraving just your wedding date on the inside of your ring,
consider following Victoria's example and adding the date of your proposal as well.

Victoria gave rings to special guests at her wedding.
You may want to consider giving rings to your attendants — or you may want to present your
mother and new mother-in-law with special rings to mark the occasion.

A custom-made gimmel ring with a secret engraving
that only you and your new husband will understand is a truly unique wedding band.

THE WEDDING DRESS

1878 1914 1923 1929

Demure, Romantic and Daring

The period from the late 1800s to the late 1920s saw a revolution in wedding dress styles. The modest fitted gowns of the late Victorian era (far left) gave way to liberated, post-war designs that featured loose-fitting dresses, often with daringly shortened hems. (Above left) Rose Fitzgerald wore a gown of satin and lace, with a Normandie lace cap and tulle veil, when she married Joseph Kennedy. (Above center) British politician Sir Anthony Eden's glamorous bride sports a "cluster" wreath, a signature bridal look during the twenties. (Above right) Shortened hemlines were offset by long trains and flowing tulle veils fashioned into tight caps on the head.

Beautiful Dresses in Exquisite Taste

Three well-known weddings showcase bridal fashion during the fifties, seventies and eighties. (Above right) Edward Kennedy's lovely bride, Joan Bennett, wore a classic satin gown and flowing lace veil at their 1958 wedding. (Right) For her 1971 White House wedding, Tricia Nixon chose a sleeveless organdy dress, with a fitted embroidered bodice, and a Juliet cap with her veil. (Left) Designer Carolina Herrera created Caroline Kennedy's 1986 satin organza gown and twenty-five-foot-long train.

A Gown fit for a Princess

(Right) Grace Kelly's magnificent gown of silk taffeta and antique Valenciennes lace — now on permanent display at the Philadelphia Museum of Art — successfully blended the classic and the romantic in an unforgettable dress that continues to influence bridal fashion today.

The style of bridal gowns has always reflected the fashion of the day

1960   *1969*   *1981*

The Height of Fashion

During the rebellious sixties, British mod fashion extended to bridal gowns — with mini wedding dresses (above left) and such free-spirited romantic creations as singer Lulu's velvet and fur-trimmed bridal ensemble (above center). Even Beatle Ringo Starr's April 1981 wedding (above right) evoked a sixties style. Only with Princess Diana's wedding later that year did bridal fashion swing back to formality, grandeur, and elegance. (Right) With its masses of soft pink petticoats, this contemporary Victorian-inspired wedding gown will enchant every bride who has dreamed of looking like a princess on her wedding day. (Far right) As we enter another century of bridal style, designers continue to take the wedding dress to new heights of fashion.

With This Ring I Thee Wed...

Not every man can pledge his troth with the dazzling diamonds Richard Burton has given to Elizabeth Taylor (left). Yet a diamond ring, no matter how small and inexpensive the stone, endures as the ultimate symbol of eternal love promised and given. Perhaps because Audrey Hepburn immortalized the famous jewelry store in the Hollywood classic, *Breakfast at Tiffany's*, a ring from Tiffany & Co. is still woven into the romantic dreams of countless young women today. In 1999, for a new generation of brides, Tiffany's introduced its Lucida diamond cut and setting (right) — a stunning tribute to contemporary romance.

CHAPTER TWO

THE GLITTER AND THE GOLD

The wedding was, without exception, the most magnificent ever celebrated in this country, which was quite fitting, in view of the great wealth and social position of the bride and the high rank of the bridegroom.

— *The New York Times,* November 7, 1895

IN THE LATE NINETEENTH and early twentieth centuries, young American heiresses were the celebrities — the supermodels and film stars — of their day. Sudden great wealth brought instant social standing in New York society for such families as the Vanderbilts, Astors, Goulds, and Whitneys. This was the era of lavish "party favors" for debutante dinner dances — little items such as pearl studs for the gentlemen and Cartier minaudières (small 18-carat gold evening purses) for the ladies. Realizing that there was a lot of social polishing to do on their family trees, the robber barons and their wives decided that foreign titles were the answer. In 1895 alone, nine famous young heiresses married British peers, marking the height of a social phenomenon that saw more than one hundred Americans with sizable dowries marrying European aristocrats in exchange for prestigious, if often impoverished, titles.

Consuelo Vanderbilt, an exquisite debutante whose father's fortune topped $200 million (equivalent to several billion today), drew the most attention. At seventeen, the tall brunette made her debut in a stunning white tulle dress at a Parisien *bal blanc* given by the Duc de Gramont. In the two months that followed the high-society ball, Consuelo received five marriage proposals. All were rejected by her ambitious mother, Alva, who was determined to add

a British lord to the family tree. Ironically, while she was busily arranging her daughter's betrothal in Paris, Alva's own stormy marriage ended. Undeterred, she and Consuelo set off for London and more titled pastures.

At a dinner party held by one of her mother's friends, Consuelo was placed beside the Duke of Marlborough, who bore one of the most illustrious names in English history. "He seemed to me very young, although six years my senior, and I thought him good-looking and intelligent," recalled Consuelo in her memoir. Nothing came of the meeting, and on her return to New York, she fell in love with Winthrop Rutherfurd, a handsome twenty-nine-year-old attorney from a distinguished American family. The day Consuelo turned eighteen they became secretly engaged. Unfortunately, Alva guessed the source of her daughter's happiness and arranged another trip to Europe, this time for five months. Although Winthrop followed the Vanderbilts to Paris, he wasn't allowed to see his distraught fiancée, and his love letters never reached her.

Following their stay in the French capital, the Vanderbilts traveled to London, where Marlborough invited them to his home for the weekend. Blenheim Palace, the only non-royal residence in England to be called a palace, is an immense house set in acres of parkland.

When Consuelo made her society debut in Paris at the age of seventeen, she was dubbed "la belle Mlle Vanderbilt au long cou," for her swanlike neck — a trademark of her beauty that is very much in evidence in this later formal portrait (opposite).

The Duke was determined to maintain the style of life his ancestors had enjoyed there, but the only way he could achieve his goal was to marry a wealthy heiress. After taking Consuelo for a drive around the estate, he must have decided she would make a suitable duchess because he accepted Alva's invitation to visit the Vanderbilts' Newport mansion in six weeks' time.

While waiting for the Duke's arrival, Consuelo was kept a prisoner at home in New York. The porter was told she was not to be allowed to leave the house unaccompanied, and the servants were ordered to give to Alva any letters she wrote. Finally, Consuelo managed to meet her lover at a ball. That night she informed Alva she had accepted Winthrop Rutherfurd's marriage proposal. Sadly, her resolve weakened the next day, when she was told by a family friend that Alva would suffer a heart attack if Consuelo continued with her plan. Brought up to obey her indomitable mother, the young heiress accepted her fate and sent word to Rutherfurd that she could not marry him.

The newly married Duchess of Marlborough hurries into a waiting carriage as thousands of curious onlookers strain to catch a glimpse of her.

On Marlborough's arrival, Consuelo accompanied him to a series of dinners and balls. At the end of his visit, the short, pompous Duke — with the inappropriate nickname of Sunny — proposed to her. "There was no need for sentiment. I was content with his pious hope that he would make me a good husband," wrote Consuelo.

November 5, 1895, was the date set for the wedding. Although it was an arranged marriage between two ill-suited people, the wedding ceremony proved to be a spectacular affair. A pink-and-white theme was chosen for the extravagant floral decorations and bouquets. At St. Thomas's Episcopal Church on Fifth Avenue, most of the woodwork was concealed with garlands of foliage and blossoms. Decorators covered the chancel rail with a trellis of fragrant lily of the valley and hung huge arrangements of pink and white roses tied with trailing ribbons to the end of every fifth pew.

The eight bridesmaids carried bouquets of pink roses and white orchids. The flowers looked wonderful against their ivory satin dresses tied with royal blue sashes. Their large velvet picture hats were each trimmed with a chiffon rosette and pale blue ostrich feathers. A choker of blue velvet, strings of pearls, and Consuelo's gift of a diamond butterfly brooch completed each bridesmaid's outfit.

In contrast, the bride wore no jewelry at all. Consuelo's cream-white satin dress needed no embellishment. The morning of her wedding she "donned the lovely lingerie with its real lace and the white silk stockings and shoes. My maid helped me into the beautiful dress, its tiers of Brussels lace cascading over white satin. It had a high collar and long tight sleeves. The court train, embroidered with seed pearls and silver, fell from my shoulders in folds of billowing whiteness. My maid fitted the tulle veil to my head with a wreath of orange blossoms; it fell over my face to my knees."

Outside the house, two thousand people waited to catch a glimpse of the famous bride leaving for the church. Consuelo admitted in her memoir that she was glad her veil protected her from the curious stares. At St. Thomas's, her father walked her slowly up the aisle to Wagner's "Bridal Chorus" from *Lohengrin* played by a sixty-member orchestra, and as Consuelo and Sunny stood solemnly at the altar, a large choir sang "O Perfect Love."

After the ceremony, a select group of guests and family members gathered at Alva's house for a sumptuous wedding breakfast. The rooms were filled with hundreds of pale pink and white orchids. At one end of the reception room, the newly married couple stood under a wedding bell of white flowers to receive their guests. For the new Duchess, it was the first of many occasions when she would perform the duties of a hostess at a party of distinguished guests.

Not surprisingly, Consuelo's marriage to the Duke of Marlborough didn't last. When I met Consuelo for tea at her home in Paris in the late forties, she was married to her true love, Jacques Balsan. She was in the waning days of her life but obviously a very happy woman. How wonderful that she eventually achieved the happiness that had eluded her so cruelly in her youth.

White slippers and white silk stockings are de rigueur, and the dainty little wedding slippers are prettiest when embroidered with rhinestones and pearls, or else finished with a very minute bow and a small jeweled buckle.

— Harper's Bazaar, 1886

THE EDWARDIAN LOOK

ALTHOUGH in reality Consuelo Vanderbilt was a late-Victorian bride, her bridal style still influenced the Edwardian era. The sophisticated look of the early 1900s was beautifully captured in the 1997 film, *Titanic*. Hair elegantly swept up, high collars encircling graceful necks, tiny waists, large picture hats, and ruffled parasols held in gloved hands characterized the fashion of the period. Lavish trim — embroidery, ribbon, flowers, fringe — decorated everything from dresses to hats.

Edwardian brides often followed the Victorian tradition of incorporating lace into their magnificent wedding gowns. The sleeves of the high-necked dress worn by Alice Roosevelt, daughter of American president Theodore Roosevelt, for her wedding in 1906 were trimmed with lace from her mother's wedding gown. She also wore a wreath of orange blossoms and a tulle veil, as Consuelo had done. Where the

Like Consuelo's wedding gown, this 1908 design also has a lace bodice, high collar and long tight sleeves. A long tulle veil, cascading from a floral wreath, completes the Edwardian bridal look.

President's daughter differed — and started a trend of her own — was in wearing a bridal gown with a long train of silver brocade. The use of silver thread and the mixing of different types of fabrics continued into the 1920s.

The lacelike platinum creations designed by jewelry artists of the day were another example of the popularity of silver. These delicate necklaces, bracelets, and earrings — along with their Art Nouveau counterparts featuring exotic flowers, dragonflies, and mythical animals — can be found at jewelers specializing in estate jewelry.

Today's Edwardian-style brides who dislike veils can chose a fantastic hat for the occasion. Somewhat scaled-down re-creations (or the full-blown article, complete with flowers, feathers, ribbons, and lace, if you want to be true to the period!) can be ordered from a specialty shop for the bride or bridesmaids. They can be particularly pretty at an afternoon wedding held outdoors. Another Edwardian standby — the shawl — has already found its way into mainstream wedding fashion.

PEARLS: A WEDDING CLASSIC

Pearl necklaces and matching earrings have always been traditional wedding jewelry. In the past, they were often given by the groom to his bride as a wedding gift. Legendary brides who have worn pearls include Queen Elizabeth, the Duchess of Kent, and Jacqueline Kennedy.

Pearls have long been known to be the most flattering jewelry next to a woman's skin. Jewelers advise brides to choose light-toned pearls if they have fair skin and cream-toned pearls if they have dark skin. If you are a bride faced with the pleasant prospect of receiving some good pearls as a wedding gift, don't worry about their length. If the necklace you receive is too long for your wedding dress, the length can be adjusted by using a "pearl shortener" where the clasp is.

Good pearl jewelry needs more care than gemstones. Wipe the pearls after you wear them to remove any hint of makeup or perfume stains, and wrap them in a piece of soft chamois to protect them from scratches.

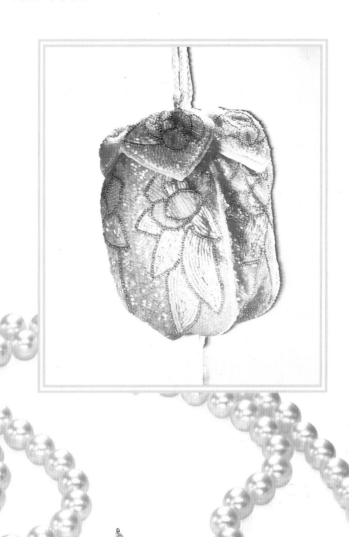

(Top) An embroidered evening bag, encrusted with a beaded bouquet of flowers, lends a romantic Edwardian touch to today's understated bridal gowns. (Above) Delicate diamond blooms add a dash of glitter to classic pearls.

INVITATION TO A WEDDING

At a formal wedding it is customary for the bride

to give her bridesmaids a few invitations, that they may have the

pleasure of sending them to personal friends.

— *The Ladies' Home Journal*, 1898

IN EUROPE, the first written wedding invitations were prepared by monks for the nobility. By the 1600s, copper-plate engraving had been invented, and the monks' script was printed in black ink to reproduce the look of calligraphy. In Consuelo's day, orders for large numbers of invitations were given to the engraver, but for an intimate wedding, it would have been considered improper to print the invitations. They would have been handwritten and hand-delivered.

Today, many stationery choices and printing options exist, including thermography, which imitates engraving, and computerized calligraphy, which reproduces the look of handwritten script. It is important to remember that an invitation to share in the joy of your wedding day is the first impression guests will have of the event. A beautiful invitation can become a prized keepsake.

The traditional formal wedding invitation features engraved lettering or calligraphy in black or dark gray ink on fine-quality white or cream-colored paper. It may or may not have a blind-embossed border. The actual text is engraved on the first page of the invitation.

Formal invitations have two envelopes to emphasize the importance of the event. The outside envelope is addressed by hand, with the sender's return address in the upper left corner and a pretty postage stamp in the upper right. The ungummed inside envelope is addressed only with the title and family name of the guest (for example, Mr. and Mrs. Jamieson). If children are invited, their given names are included below their parents' names. Children who are over the age of eighteen should be sent their own invitations.

The most informal wedding invitation, obviously to a small event, is the personal letter written on good notepaper, giving the date, time, and place, RSVP information, and adding, "It would mean so much to us to have you with us for this important moment." Another informal way to extend a wedding invitation is to print the formal text on a single sheet of good-quality stationery. White or cream stock is the traditional choice, but today all kinds of colors and interesting papers, including the rice papers of the Far East, are part of the design scheme.

Always order at least twenty-five more invitations than you think you will need. Some may be spoiled at the engravers or damaged in transit to you. Inevitably, couples forget older relatives, a retired boss, or college roommates with whom they have lost touch. Even though you know these people cannot come to your wedding, they would probably be delighted to receive an invitation.

Formal wedding announcements, engraved on the same stock as the wedding invitation and enclosing the couple's At-Home card (with their address, telephone number, and e-mail address), are sent to people who were not invited to the wedding but with whom the bridal couple wishes to share the good news. The recipients are not expected to send a gift, but good friends always do, as a sign of affection for the couple. Wedding announcements are mailed after the wedding ceremony has taken place, not one minute before.

All your wedding stationery should be ordered at the same time to save time and money. In addition to invitations and announcements, you may want to order thank-you notes, place cards for the reception, rehearsal-dinner invitations, and a weekend wedding program used to advise guests of planned activities, appropriate attire, and travel and accommodation arrangements.

(Opposite) Although cream and white paper stocks are still the traditional choices for wedding invitations, envelopes in a contrasting color — with matching ink on the invitation — are popular among many young couples.

Mr. and Mrs. Michael Appleton

invite you to celebrate

the marriage of his daughter

DINA ALYSE

to

JEAN-CHRISTOPHE

son of Mr. Yves and Dr. Danielle Carron-Daguet

Sunday, the second of July

Two thousand

o'clock in the evening

ario Museum

ISSUING THE INVITATION

The etiquette for issuing wedding invitations has changed in the past twenty years for several reasons, including an increase in inter-faith marriages and in the number of people remarrying.

❦ In a traditional formal invitation to a Christian wedding, names are given in full:

Mr. and Mrs. George Lesley Jordan
request the honour of your presence
at the marriage of their daughter
Theresa Anne
to
Mr. Russell William Strickland

The bride's family name is not given because her parents are issuing the invitation and their family name is already present. The names of the groom's parents are not on the invitation, so his family name is included.

❦ If Mrs. Jordan uses her maiden name, the hosts' names would appear on one line:

Mr. George Lesley Jordan and Ms. Anne Reid Elliott

❦ If the Jordans are divorced, and she has remarried, their names would appear separately on two lines:

Mrs. Anthony Taylor Smithton
and
Mr. George Lesley Jordan

❦ Today many women use their maiden name after a divorce. In this case, the invitation would read:

Ms. Anne Reid Elliott
and
Mr. George Lesley Jordan

THE CONTENTS OF THE ENVELOPE

Aside from the invitation itself, the inside envelope may contain a number of enclosures.

❦ RECEPTION CARD. This card is included if the reception is not being held in the same place as the ceremony.

❦ CEREMONY CARD. Enclose this card if all your guests will be attending the reception but only a few will be invited to the ceremony.

❦ REPLY CARD. This card and a self-addressed stamped envelope are much more commonly used today than the letters "RSVP" placed in the lower left corner of formal invitations. Single people who have been invited to bring an escort should write the name of this person on the reply card.

❦ MAP CARD. A map card is included when necessary to show guests how to find the place of worship or the reception venue.

❦ DIRECTIONS CARD. Used when a map is not necessary but when written directions giving highway and freeway exits might be useful. If valet parking will be available at the reception, state that welcome information here.

❦ PEW CARD. A pew card is enclosed when some of the pews at a very large formal wedding will be reserved for special guests. This card should be brought to the ceremony.

❦ RAIN CARD. Indicates an alternative location for an outdoor wedding in case of bad weather (include a telephone number to call for information).

❦ AT-HOME CARD. Gives the couple's address, telephone number and the date they will be moving into their new home, if they are not already living together.

❦ To stuff the cards into the inner envelope, the reception card is inserted after the invitation itself, the reply card follows, lying face up within the flap of its envelope, and any other cards are the final insertions. If the invitation is folded, smaller pieces are tucked inside it.

❧ An older couple, or a couple who has been married before, issues the invitation in their own names:

Bettina Adams Verde
and
Jonathan Watriss Miller

❧ If either of the bride's parents has a professional title, he or she may certainly use it on a formal wedding invitation:

Mr. Eric Chanterelle and Dr. Mary Chase

❧ The bride may want her stepfather to take over the role of "father of the bride" at her wedding, particularly if her natural father has not played a role in her life. Traditionally, the father of the bride's name should appear with the mother's on the invitation but, depending on circumstances, this is perhaps a time when the rules should be broken, allowing the stepfather's name to appear alongside the mother's name.

❧ For a Christian wedding, only the parents of the bride are listed as the hosts, while for a Jewish wedding, both sets of parents are listed. What appears on the invitation when a Christian woman marries a Jewish man? According to the wishes of the couple and/or their parents, both sets of parents or the bride's parents only can be the issuers of the invitation.

❧ The date, year, and time of the wedding, as well as words such as "street" and "avenue," are not abbreviated.

❧ The phrase "request the honour of your presence" is used when the ceremony takes place in a house of worship. (English spellings are commonly used as a matter of tradition.) When the wedding takes place in a home, hotel, or other location, the phrase "request the pleasure of your company" is more correct than asking for the honour of their presence.

Today couples are sending out invitations containing bits of love poetry, lyrics from songs, and touching love sonnets they have written themselves. We are in a period of immense creativity and social change, and manners must reflect the state of the world today, not yesterday. But perhaps there should be a word of caution here to brides and grooms that the tried-and-true way of issuing wedding invitations has a great deal of merit. There is a reason for all those rules. Traditional invitations communicate what is to happen, when, where, and how in a gracious, formal way, in keeping with the importance of the event.

THE WEDDING BREAKFAST

For the wedding breakfast the bridal party, consisting of eighteen guests,
sat at an oval-shaped table set in the dining room. . . . Running down the center of
the table was a solid blanket of white orchids and lilies of the valley, with a
border of smilax. The candelabra had shades of white silk.

— *The New York Times*, November 7, 1895

Consuelo Vanderbilt and Queen Victoria both had wedding breakfasts, which today we would call brunches or luncheons. Louis Sherry, New York's leading caterer of the day, provided "breakfast" for one hundred and fifteen wedding guests at Alva Vanderbilt's Fifth Avenue mansion at 1:30 in the afternoon. The menu included dishes such as Eggs on Toast with Tarragon-Infused Brown Sauce and Turban of Tropical Fruit with Cardamom Yogurt Sauce.

Although Sherry's dishes are probably too rich for today's tastes, an Edwardian-inspired wedding breakfast might feature an asparagus-and-goat-cheese tart, roasted sea bass, veal medallions, and salads decorated with edible flowers. Attractive period touches might include traditional china, crystal, and silver, white lace or linen tablecloths, and epergnes — towering tiered centerpieces overflowing with lavish displays of fruit and flowers, copied from the displays seen by newly rich Americans on their "grand tours" of Europe. At the 1906 White House wedding of President Theodore Roosevelt's daughter, Alice, the epergnes on the tables were laden with strawberries, grapes, and a new species of pear named "Princess Alice" in her honor.

Whether traditional dishes or the very latest in food trends are served at your breakfast, it is a thoughtful idea to provide canapés and something to drink while you are greeting your guests and before everyone sits down to eat. Hard-cooked quail's eggs topped with caviar are an Edwardian-inspired choice, but miniature crabcakes or mini bagels with interesting spreads such as baba ghanouj are a tasty modern alternative. Offer an espresso and cappuccino bar or pitchers of chai tea (both coffee and tea can be iced for hot-weather appeal) as well as trays of freshly squeezed fruit juices, sparkling water, mimosas, white-wine sangria, or Bloody Marys.

(Above) The Edwardians' love of silver — in serving dishes, dessert trays, and coffee services — is evident in this period illustration of a wedding breakfast. Garlands cascading from slender silver vases create a charming maypole effect that adds to the splendor of the table.

A PERFECTLY CATERED AFFAIR

THE IDEAL WEDDING caterer provides wonderful reception food served by a well-trained, properly dressed wait staff. Here is what an experienced caterer should be able to provide.

❧ IDEAS. The caterer should be able to give you suggestions for a reception based on your wishes, price limitations, and his or her capabilities. He or she should be able to take your wedding planner of ideas and realistically try to accommodate you. However, don't expect the caterer to produce perfect dishes from recipes you supply. It is much safer to go with dishes that the caterer has made successfully before.

❧ PAST RECORD. Sample menus and photographs of dishes and table displays that the caterer has supplied for past weddings should be available for you to see.

❧ SPECIAL DIETS. Choose a menu that includes rice and several vegetables to accommodate people who are vegetarian or on special diets.

❧ TASTING. A tasting should be arranged several weeks in advance of the wedding to iron out any concerns about flavors, presentation, or portion size.

❧ SCHEDULE. It is wise to have a plan of action written out for everything from valet-parking arrangements to checking coats. A schedule should list when the drinks and canapés will be served, when the food will be served, when the cake will be cut, and when the bar will be closed. If musicians have been hired to play at the reception, a copy of this schedule should be given to them.

❧ WRITTEN AGREEMENT. A written agreement should cover such items as the date and time of the reception, the address of the reception site, the amount to be paid upon signing, services included in the price, an itemized menu, the number of guests, the number of meals (counting extra meals for the photographer, musicians, etc.), the number of wait staff (there should be at least one server for every twenty guests at a buffet reception, and one server for every eight guests at a sit-down meal), what the servers will wear, the time the meal will be served, cake-cutting fees, guidelines for the bar, liquor-license fees, overtime fees, gratuity (if included in the quotation), cleanup procedures, and the terms of payment.

❧ MARKUP. This is the caterer's charge for rented linens, china, glassware, and cutlery (it may be cheaper for you to rent these yourself).

❧ INSURANCE. The caterer should be able to provide a certificate of insurance for enough liability to cover the reception venue.

❧ DEPOSIT FEE. This is usually 25 to 50 percent of the caterer's final fee, and is paid on booking (balance is paid approximately ten days before the reception).

SELF-CATERING AT A SMALL HOME WEDDING

The following tips will help you plan your own reception at home.

❧ NEIGHBORS. Remember to warn your neighbors about the reception well in advance. They will be less disturbed if they know beforehand. A gift of some wedding flowers sent to their houses also softens any irritations.

❧ ASSISTANCE. It is impossible to do it alone. At least three people are needed to act as bartender, server, and cleanup person. Assign duties and draw up a time line for the entire reception. Meet with the hired staff or volunteers well before the event and discuss how the day will unfold.

❧ RECIPES. If you are going to use a new recipe, make it for your family or friends twice before the wedding so you know that it is not only delicious but also manageable in your kitchen.

❧ RENTALS. Estimate how many serving utensils, bowls, and platters will be needed, and arrange to rent or borrow them. Rent as much as your budget permits, because dishes, glasses, cutlery, and linens can be returned without being washed. Large worktables can also be rented so that the kitchen staff has plenty of room to assemble the food. Order 5 to 10 percent more linen and glassware than you think you will need, to guard against the unexpected. If you borrow equipment, platters, or linen from friends and relatives, be sure to keep a list of what belongs to whom.

CAKES: A SWEET CELEBRATION

In the lower hall were two tables, on one of which was placed the white boxes containing the wedding cake, and on the other floral favors consisting of corsage bouquets for the women and boutonnieres for the men.

— *The New York Times*, November 7, 1895

MORE THAN ANY other visual element, the cake has come to symbolize the wedding. At a little girl's tea party I once attended, each of the guests was served a tiny cupcake made by the ten-year-old hostess. The cakes were all beautifully decorated, and when I remarked on this, our hostess said, "Oh, I'm just practicing for my wedding. I'm going to bake my own wedding cake when I get married."

Sharing food in celebration is a well-loved practice, and a wedding cake in some shape or form has been present at marriage ceremonies since the days of the ancient Greeks. Consuelo Vanderbilt, like many of her contemporaries, followed the wedding traditions begun by Queen Victoria. The elaborate cakes of this period, however, can be traced to the 1858 wedding of Victoria's daughter, the Princess Royal. Instead of an immense one-layer cake, the royal bakers constructed a three-tiered cake rising six feet into the air — the first wedding cake of its kind.

As the century progressed, these towering white confections grew more and more ornate. Flowers remained the favorite garnish — in particular, the romantic rose. Fresh roses were used to decorate the frosting, and rosewater and syrup were beaten into the batter. (Rosewater in food or drink was said to bind a husband to his wife.) Spun-sugar lace, latticework, vines, and flowers covered every available inch of the cake, while cloth ribbons hung over the sides, and a vase of fresh or gum-paste flowers stood at the very top.

The bride's cake, which was generally a lightly spiced white cake, did not appear until the 1890s. Until then, wedding cakes were elaborately iced fruitcakes. These survived as the groom's cake, which was packed ahead into small white boxes and given to guests as they left the reception.

In later years, the white-frosted, tiered wedding cake appeared on most reception tables. At the 1966 White House wedding of Luci Baines Johnson, daughter of President Lyndon B. Johnson, a traditional light fruitcake made up six layers

Whether you choose a
classic white-frosted cake adorned
with fresh or gum-paste flowers,
or splurge on an architectural
extravaganza, make sure your
cake is in keeping with the mood
and setting of the reception
you've planned.

of the cake, but the seventh layer was the bride's favorite chocolate cake. She and her husband, Patrick Nugent, carried the "bride's cake" away with them on their honeymoon.

Wedding cakes today range from the tiered cakes of old and the cascade cakes popular in the eighties to individual cupcakes cleverly arranged on a tiered cake plate to look like a wedding cake. Artists like Sylvia Weinstock, Gail Watson and Cile Bellefleur-Burbidge create realistic-looking blossoms, ribbons, and flourishes for their fantasies of cake and frosting, while other bakers decorate their cakes with beautiful organic flowers, using the same varieties as in the bridal bouquet. At truly extravagant weddings, miniature versions of the cake are served to guests at the reception. Whatever your budget, a magical cake can be found to share with your guests.

CUTTING THE CAKE

Until the 1930s, it was considered the bride's duty to cut the wedding cake and distribute small pieces to the guests. It was her first act as a married woman. But as the cakes have become more elaborate and the icing difficult to cut through, the task of cutting the cake has become a joint one. The knife is held in the bride's right hand, the groom's right hand covers hers, and her left hand is placed on top. The bride is the first to take a bite of the piece they have cut together. She then feeds the groom the second bite.

(Right) Inspired by the grand creations of the past, this elaborately decorated confection features handpainted royal icing, gum-paste fruits, flowers, and butterflies — and for the crowning touch, a gum-paste bouquet in an ornate vase made of handpainted molded sugar.

CAKE BOXES

Traditionally, the cake was cut into small pieces and packed into little white boxes as a souvenir for wedding guests. Women interested in marrying would sometimes slip their piece of cake under their pillow for good luck, hoping they would see the face of their future husband in their dreams. In England, the boxes were sent to friends and relatives unable to attend the

celebration as a way of sharing the luck of the wedding with loved ones. Today, these special square or heart-shaped boxes are still available from wedding suppliers or box manufacturers. When cake boxes are planned for a wedding, a slab cake — in addition to the wedding cake — is baked and decorated. Small pieces of this cake, or specially made little cakes, are placed in the boxes and delivered to the reception site with the wedding cake.

CHOOSING A WEDDING CAKE

As always, recommendations from friends are a good way to find the right baker for your wedding cake. The best people make works of art, which taste wonderful and are made from fresh ingredients, not a mix. Long gone are the days when one expected a wedding cake to taste dry and uninteresting.

Before visiting the cakemaker, you will need to know the number of people attending the reception and the type of reception it will be. A reputable baker or caterer will be happy to show you photographs of past work. He or she will also arrange for a tasting of two or three flavors. You will be asked whether you want to keep the top layer of the cake for your first anniversary or first christening, or whether you want to take it with you on the honeymoon. (Some bakers will bake a duplicate of the top layer for you on your anniversary rather than have the cake layer frozen for a year.)

To save money, some couples order a small wedding cake and several sheet cakes made in the same flavor and with the same frosting. This also helps speed up the serving of the cake. Since the cake is usually removed by the caterer to another room for slicing, no one need know that a sheet cake is being used.

It's a good idea to get the details in writing.
Here are some questions for the baker to answer before you make a commitment:

❧ What does he or she consider a serving size? Some suppliers have a larger size if the cake is to be served as the only dessert.

❧ When will the cake be baked? If the cakemaker doesn't plan to freeze the cake, it should be baked one day, or two days at most, before the wedding.

❧ Can it be made with fresh fruit in season? Choosing fruit in season will help keep costs down.

❧ What kinds of cake and what flavors are available? Is the cake made from fresh ingredients?

❧ Will the cake be delivered in a refrigerated vehicle? This is an issue only when an amateur cakemaker has been hired to make the cake.

❧ What kinds of frosting are offered? Buttercream does not hold up well at outdoor summer wedding receptions or at indoor locales that are not air conditioned. Rolled fondant is better.

❧ What kinds of garnishes and sauces are offered to make each dessert plate look special? All edible garnishes should relate to the contents of the cake — for example, an orange chiffon cake might have frosted ornamental oranges.

❧ Does the price include delivery and setup?

WEDDING FAVORS

While the contract was being signed, the bridesmaids walked slowly down the central aisle and handed pink and white posies to those seated. . . .

— *The New York Times*, November 7, 1895

EVERY GUEST appreciates being presented with a token to remember a couple's wedding day. The tradition stems from the old belief that the good fortune of the wedding feast should be shared with guests by giving them a gift of food to take home at the end of the celebration. At the 1923 wedding of Lady Elizabeth Bowes-Lyon (now the Queen Mother) to the future king, George VI, guests were given patisserie in small spun-sugar baskets. In 1959, the Crown Prince of Japan and Princess Michiko presented their guests with beautifully decorated wooden boxes tied with red and white silk cords. Inside each box were such delicacies as salmon galantine and sweet chestnuts.

Bomboniere, usually wrapped in white or pastel tulle, belong to the Italian wedding tradition. Each of these favors contains five sugared almonds symbolizing health, wealth, happiness, fertility, and long life. Each is personalized by a small card with the bride's and groom's first name, and the date of the wedding.

In addition to gifts of food, flower and ribbon favors have been popular since Elizabethan times. Queen Victoria's bridesmaids handed out white satin ribbons tied with silver lace. Consuelo Vanderbilt's attendants distributed pink and white nosegays to guests at the church, and those invited to the reception were given a flower favor to take home.

Wedding favors, no matter how small, should reflect a couple's personality and style. Although handmade gifts are wonderful, if making them isn't a labor of love, it's better to buy good-quality favors. You can add a personal touch by strolling with your new husband from table to table at the reception as the wedding cake is being served, passing out the wedding favors from a pretty basket. Or the favors can be attractively laid out on a table with a handwritten card inviting guests to take one home.

PLEASE TAKE HOME. . .

- ❧ Beautifully packaged chocolates, peanut brittle, or fudge
- ❧ Bottles of homemade or store-bought wine with personalized labels
- ❧ Tiny potted plants
- ❧ Tiny books of love poetry

- ❧ Homemade preserves, sundae sauce, or other treats in decorative containers
- ❧ Decorated candles or candle holders
- ❧ Pretty fans for an outdoor summer wedding

- ❧ Small frames, used as place-card holders at the reception and given to guests after the wedding
- ❧ Floral potpourri sachets that incorporate the flowers used in the bouquets and centerpieces

- ❧ In springtime, fancy gardening tags fastened to a packet of seeds featuring the flowers in the bridal bouquet
- ❧ In autumn, a package of bulbs that will bloom in the spring, reminding guests of your wedding

Something Borrowed

Although we would consider the decoration of the church at Consuelo's wedding excessive
by today's standards, a nineteenth-century blossom-covered garden trellis at the entrance to the
center aisle of seats can make a lovely focus for a church or garden setting.

For an Edwardian-style wedding, large picture hats trimmed
with flowers are very romantic and almost always flattering on the bridesmaids.
The bride should order the hats and pay for them.

If you love silver, you might incorporate it into your gown or a luxurious wrap.
Delicate Edwardian jewelry is the ideal accessory. Or consider a hint of silver in the ribbon of a
bouquet, the trim of a napkin, or the candlesticks on the tables at the reception.

Butterflies never go out of fashion. Although Consuelo's
gift of diamond butterfly brooches to her attendants would be feasible
today only for the daughter of a very wealthy couple, small enamel
and sterling-silver butterflies with semiprecious stones can be readily found,
and custom jewelry pieces, including hairpins and brooches,
can be ordered from jewelry designers.

A pretty bridal wreath of white flowers was the only accessory Consuelo wore.
For those who don't like jewelry, this simple, beautiful look is an option worth considering.

The use of china, crystal, silver, and white lace or linen tablecloths
can lend an elegant feel to a wedding breakfast. Other Edwardian touches could include
old-fashioned epergnes of fresh or sugared fruit, and a blanket of flowers running
down the middle of the wedding table.

A small vase of flowers set into the top of the wedding cake
is an Edwardian touch that solves the problem of adding real flowers to a cake when organic,
pesticide-free blooms are hard to find.

THE WEDDING CAKE

Victorian & Edwardian Cakes

(Left and below) Elaborate decoration was the hallmark of wedding cakes during the Victorian and Edwardian periods. Spun-sugar lace, latticework, vines, and flowers covered every available inch of the cake, and a vase of fresh or gum-paste flowers often stood on the top. These ornate architectural fantasies — recreated here by master cake designer Cile Bellefleur-Burbidge — held place of honor at the wedding breakfast and were often inspired by dazzling Dresden china centerpieces created for European royalty.

1941   *1945*   *1953*

Gloria Vanderbilt (Above left) The 17-year-old heiress's four-tiered wedding cake featured a large cake topper, complete with a bride dressed in a miniature version of Ms. Vanderbilt's gown and long veil.

Bette Davis (Above center) The always elegant actress and her husband, William Grant Sherry, smile for the cameras as they prepare to cut their wedding cake.

John & Jacqueline Kennedy (Above right) Ambassador Joseph Kennedy commissioned an Irish bakery in Quincy, Massachusetts, to create the four-foot-high, five-tiered cake for "the wedding of the year." Elaborately iced with swirls and hearts, the top tier of the cake held a bouquet of fresh miniature roses. Jackie went through two different cake-cutting ceremonies to please the multitude of photographers who kept clamoring for shots of the dashing young senator and his beautiful bride.

The Artful Cake (Left) As romantic as the painting that inspired it, this contemporary edible masterpiece by Santa Fe baker-designer Cliff Simon recreates Chagall's *The Three Candles* on a canvas of icing and cake.

Paul Newman & Joanne Woodward

(Below left) A simple wedding cake seemed appropriate when one of Hollywood's most romantic couples tied the knot during a secret wedding ceremony in Las Vegas.

Elvis & Priscilla Presley

(Below right) As thousands of teenage girls mourned the loss of the world's most eligible bachelor, Elvis Presley and his bride cut their towering multi-tiered wedding cake.

2000

1958   1967

Let Them Eat Cake!

Today's wedding cakes play a starring role at the reception, and their design reflects not only the style of the bride and groom but also the kind of reception they've planned. Some newlyweds are opting for individual cakes (above) to serve each guest. Although these tiny tiered creations are more expensive per person than a slice of a larger cake, the effect is spectacular — and many guests choose to take their mini cakes home to enjoy the next day. Equally spectacular are couture cakes, such as this signature pale yellow and white floral masterpiece (below left) by legendary cake-maker Sylvia Weinstock, or simpler cakes adorned with fresh flowers (below right) that match the bouquets of the bridal party.

A Royal Wedding Cake

(Right) Chief Petty Officer David Avery, a master baker at the Royal Navy's Chatham Dockyard, oversaw the creation of Charles and Diana's wedding cake in 1981. The five-tiered confection — containing fifty pounds of marzipan, forty-nine pounds of white icing, and a quarter-pint of dark naval rum — featured a miniature bridal bouquet of white flowers, grapes for prosperity, and doves for peace and happiness.

CHAPTER THREE

LOVE SPEAKS IN FLOWERS

I asked Constance Spry, the prominent London florist, to come to

Candé to do the flowers for the wedding. . . . She brought her assistant with her,

and in a matter of hours they had transformed the atmosphere of the house. . . .

This was her wedding present to me.

— from the Duchess of Windsor's memoirs

IN THE SPRING of 1937, Wallis Warfield Simpson looked out over the French countryside, its fields gaily edged with lilacs and dotted with flowering fruit trees and the extravagant white blossoms of chestnuts. In a few days, she would be marrying the English king who had given up his throne for her.

Wallis remembered first meeting Edward, who was then Prince of Wales, in 1930 at a party in an English country house. She was married to her second husband, Ernest Simpson, an American with close family and business ties to England. The socially ambitious couple had entered fully into the glittering, high-society life of 1920s London. Wallis's sleek, elegant appearance and her witty conversation and surprising bursts of laughter made her a popular houseguest and increasingly drew the future King of England to her side. An invitation to the Prince's country retreat, Fort Belvedere, for the weekend of January 30, 1932, was the beginning of a relationship that would culminate in one of the most romantic, yet scandalous, love affairs of the twentieth century.

The Simpsons soon became part of the Prince's inner circle of friends. Wallis entranced him by not fawning over him. Ignoring royal etiquette, she treated the most eligible bachelor in the world like any other man — calling him David, letting him light her cigarettes for her, preceding him through doorways. By early 1934, when Wallis was thirty-seven, she wrote that they had passed "the indefinable boundary between friendship and love."

Two years later, on January 21, 1936, George V died, and the Prince of Wales, at the age of forty-two, became the new ruler, Edward VIII.

During the following weeks, Wallis began divorce proceedings. The King had not mentioned marriage to her until a dinner party for Prime Minister Stanley Baldwin was being discussed. Wallis, who not surprisingly had been greeted with coolness by the members of the Royal Family she had met, didn't think she should attend. But the King told her matter-of-factly, "It's got to be done. Sooner or later my prime minister must meet my future wife."

(Opposite) This 1936 watercolor by Cecil Beaton was painted less than three weeks before Edward VIII signed the Instrument of Abdication. Wallis wears the Van Cleef & Arpels ruby and diamond necklace the King had given her for her fortieth birthday earlier that year.

A BRIDE AGAIN

*I*F, LIKE WALLIS Simpson, you are marrying again, the following advice will help you hold a memorable wedding in the best of taste. The ceremony itself should be small and should include only family and your closest friends. Your larger circle of friends should be invited to the reception, which may be as large and lavish as you wish. Invitations to the ceremony are usually extended by the bride or groom in a personal note or telephone call. Engraved or printed invitations to the reception are sent by the bride and groom, unless the bride is very young, in which case her parents once again invite the guests to the reception.

Some women who weren't able to be married with all the fuss the first time long to fulfill their wedding fantasies the second time. But if you wish to remarry according to traditional etiquette, there are certain things you should avoid. For example, parties given for the two of you should not be called "engagement" parties, since a woman who is remarrying does not go through an engagement period. Wearing a long white bridal dress with a train and veil is, strictly speaking, not appropriate, nor is a galaxy of bridesmaids. A long or short gown of an off-white, silver-gray, or any pastel color or print is suitable. As for the attendants, there should be one for the bride and one for the groom. A child from a former marriage may stand up for a parent, provided he or she is a teenager and is mature enough to understand the significance of the marriage ceremony.

At the ceremony, there is no processional or recessional; the guests simply seat themselves, and as the bride, you are not given away again by your father. In a place of worship, your attendant precedes you as you walk unescorted from the side of the building to the center of the altar area to join your groom and his attendant. The ceremony is usually short, often informal, and almost always, in this kind of intimate environment, very touching and memorable.

The coronation was set for May 12, 1937, and the King was determined to marry Wallis as soon as possible after her divorce so that she would be at his side during the celebration. At that time, there was nothing in the British Constitution to prevent the King from marrying this soon-to-be-twice-divorced American woman. However, the King could not bring the Crown into controversy, particularly political controversy. Unfortunately, this was exactly what he did. As Edward rushed ahead with his plans, opposition to the marriage mounted and placed the government at odds with the Crown. Finally, on December 10, 1936, the King had no choice but to abdicate.

The following evening, in a solemn radio address to his former subjects, he said, "You must believe me when I tell you that I have found it impossible to carry the heavy burden of responsibility and to discharge my duties as King as I would wish to do without the help and support of the woman I love." Wallis, who had fled to

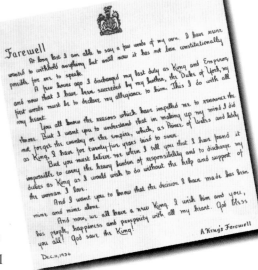

Cannes to escape death threats from an angry English public, listened sadly to her fiancé's words over the crackling French radio. Nearly five months later, the couple listened together as the coronation of George VI, the ex-King's brother, was broadcast around the world. Afterward, the newly titled Duke of Windsor turned to Wallis and tenderly said, "You must have no regrets — I have none. This much I know: what I know of happiness is forever associated with you."

Their wedding date was set for June 3 at the Château de Candé, a romantic sixteenth-century estate set on a high hill

(Above) "A King's Farewell," the broadcast made by Edward VIII to his former subjects on December 11, 1936, is printed on a commemorative silk handkerchief. (Opposite) A portrait by Cecil Beaton on the grounds of the Château de Candé, taken a few weeks before the wedding.

(Inset) Constance Spry's magnificent floral arrangements adorn the entrance to the salon where the wedding ceremony was to take place. Wallis stands in front of the makeshift altar, wearing the signature Mainbocher dress — christened "Wallis blue" by the press — that was immediately copied and sold around the world. (Background) A section of the linen tablecloth that covered the altar.

I'll make my life with you outside the boundaries of a nationality.

Nothing is going to crush me — not the British Empire, not the American press.

You and I will make a life together, a good life.

— Wallis Simpson, in a note to Edward

overlooking a lake in the Loire Valley. Inside, owners Fern and Charles Bedaux had softened the château's feudal appearance with rich draperies and hangings, soft lighting, and Louis XVI furniture. Every luxury was provided for the small party of wedding guests, including baths fragrant with the scent of red carnations.

Cecil Beaton, the famous English photographer, had visited a few weeks before the ceremony to take informal pictures. A hairdresser and manicurist worked their magic, and then Wallis joined Beaton outside. One of the settings they chose was a shady spot under the trees where daisies covered the grass. The couple considered their numerous dogs part of the family, and a passing greyhound was pressed into service. "The photography went on for many hours," remembered Beaton. "Birds sang; conditions, and settings and organdie dresses were ideal."

Beaton returned again the day before the wedding to find dozens of journalists waiting outside the gates. Society florist Constance Spry and her assistant, both wearing white overalls and large hats, bustled about decorating the château. Everywhere, there were mountains of fragrant Madonna lilies, syringa, laurel, and other ethereal white blooms. Spry, who was known for her brilliant floral arrangements, had happily come from London to convert the gloomy château into a glorious bower. She was utterly devoted to the bride, and understood how important beautiful flowers were to Wallis — whether one exquisite gardenia set in a cut-glass vase on a dressing table or sprays of white orchids and arums displayed in a hallway.

The wedding was to take place in the small but sun-filled music room, where the piano had been removed and replaced with chairs for the sixteen guests. An ornate chest was moved from a hallway and covered with a delicate linen tablecloth, embroidered with ivy leaves and berries, to serve as an altar. Two enormous floral arrangements were positioned at each side of the room, marking an entrance to the candlelit altar area. Cecil Beaton remembers, "The air [was] heavy with the scent of lily of the valley and white peonies."

Toward noon, the guests were taken to a neighboring village for lunch so that Beaton could photograph the bride and groom in their wedding clothes. The Duke appeared first. Always impeccably dressed, he had changed into a morning coat, a white carnation in his buttonhole. When Wallis appeared, he said, "Oh, so this is the great dress? Well, it's lovely, very pretty."

Wallis later wrote, "Like any other woman who had been married before, my idea was to have a perfectly simple dress and a perfectly simple hat to go with it." The dress, of an unusual pale blue crepe satin, had been dyed to match the color of the salon where the wedding was to be held. Over it, Wallis wore a tightly fitted long-sleeved jacket with tiny buttons on the midriff to accentuate her incredible slimness. The outfit had been created by the American designer Mainbocher, who had worked on it at Candé for six successive Saturdays. Women the world over copied the dress, usually with disastrous results, because very few of them had Wallis's taut, flat midriff, and dressmakers were unable to recreate the intricate pattern of folds on the bodice.

At Wallis's throat sparkled an Art Deco-style sapphire-and-diamond brooch. A pink-and-blue feathered straw hat crowned the bride's head, and blue suede shoes with three-inch heels peeked out from beneath the softly flared skirt. Wallis's short gloves matched her dress, the fourth finger slit to allow the Duke to slip on the wedding ring. On one wrist she wore a sapphire-and-diamond bracelet, a gift from her beloved.

The next day, the couple dressed in their wedding clothes again in preparation for the ceremony at noon. The well-known French organist Marcel Dupré played Bach's Cantata no. 29, Schumann's Canon in B minor, one of his own compositions, and "O Perfect Love." A civil ceremony performed by the local mayor preceded the religious ceremony, which was officiated by an obscure English clergyman who had offered his services at the last moment, much to the chagrin of his bishop. (Church of England clergy were not allowed to marry divorced persons.) With tears in his eyes, the Duke slipped the wedding band of rare Welsh gold on Wallis's finger. It was engraved "Wallis 18-10-35 Your David 3-6-37" — the first date, his official proposal to her, and the second, their wedding day.

Champagne toasts and a simple buffet luncheon of chicken à la king, French pastries, and wild strawberries and cream followed the ceremony. The fact that the wedding buffet featured chicken à la king is interesting gastronomically because, thanks to the Windsor wedding, this dish became the most favored luncheon main course offered by American hostesses over the next three decades. An updated version of it would feature a reduced cream sauce rather than the thick white sauce used in the past.

After the meal, Edward served everyone the Wallis Cocktail — a mixture of Cointreau, gin, lemon juice, peppermint, and soda — which he had created in his new wife's honor. Later that afternoon, the Duke and Duchess of Windsor began their journey south for their summer-long honeymoon in Venice. Their intimate wedding had epitomized what would become known as The Windsor Style — carefully controlled elegance that marked the couple's clothing and surroundings throughout their life together.

(Above) A small memento of their historic union, this white silk-covered box was inscribed by the newlyweds: "A piece of our wedding cake WE WE 3-VI-37." (Left) A newsreel photographer captures a very happy Duchess of Windsor, with the Duke and several guests, shortly after the wedding ceremony. (Right) The Château de Candé.

THE BRIDAL BOUQUET

I'm going to make the flowers as beautiful as I can. . . . I'd do anything for her. I adore her.

— Constance Spry,
Wallis Simpson's floral designer, 1937

CONSTANCE SPRY loved white flowers, particularly for weddings. She admired the interplay of light and shade, color, and shape in a white bouquet. In this, the innovative floral designer agreed with her Victorian predecessors.

The fragrant white orange blossom, a traditional symbol of fertility and good fortune in marriage, adorned every Victorian bride. In fact, it was considered improper to wear or carry this flower at any other time. Many large Victorian gardens had orangeries, but in later years the blossoms had to be imported or reproduced in wax. As late as the 1920s, Spry remembers seeing "a large formal posy composed entirely of orange blossom and its buds, surrounded by a frill of white paper and tied with white ribbon — Victorian, delightful and entirely romantic." These charming circular nosegays were very popular in Victoria's time, when sending messages using the language of flowers was at its height. Each flower had its own meaning: baby's breath signified fertility; bachelor button, hope; calla lily, beauty; carnation, bonds of affection; daisy, innocence; purple lilac, first love; lily of the valley, return of happiness; rose, love; and sweet pea, pleasure.

In addition to orange blossom, tiny lily of the valley, lush roses, and exotic orchids played a part in the nineteenth-century wedding. Although Victoria carried a small posy made up solely of

(Above) The knotted satin ribbons cascading from this Edwardian-style shower bouquet symbolize
the union of husband and wife, and are believed to bring luck to a marriage. (Right) Romance, simplicity and elegance —
all are captured beautifully in this understated bouquet of white roses in half bloom.

BOUQUET STYLES

Over the years, floral designers have created bouquet styles ranging from loosely massed blooms to tightly arranged posies.

❧ CASCADE. A teardrop-shaped collection of blossoms that cascades from a main grouping to fewer and smaller flowers toward the end of the bouquet.

❧ NOSEGAY. A small, round tight bouquet, sometimes backed with tulle, lace, or paper. Also known as a posy or a hand-tied bouquet.

❧ ARM (SHEAF). Long-stemmed flowers, such as delphiniums, lilacs, and lilies, tied together with ribbon and carried in the crook of one arm.

❧ BIEDERMEIER. A posy with carefully arranged concentric circles of colored flowers, each ring containing one type of flower.

❧ CRESCENT. A small central grouping of blooms with a spray trailing down on either side to form a crescent shape.

❧ COMPOSITE-FLOWER. One large bloom made from the petals of many blossoms.

❧ SPECIALTY. Flowers attached to a prayer book, fan, or muff, or arranged in a handled basket.

snowdrops (Prince Albert's favorite flower), the bouquet of her great-great-great granddaughter, Princess Anne, contained all of the traditional bridal flowers — fifteen white roses, fifty lily of the valley, several white orchids, and the modern substitute for orange blossom, stephanotis.

In the Edwardian era, sumptuous shower bouquets combined roses and ribbons in a luxurious "rain" of flowers. Tiny buds and blossoms were knotted at intervals along lengths of satin ribbon falling from the main bouquet. Knots, an ancient symbol of the union of husband and wife, were believed to bring luck to a marriage. After the ceremony, Edwardian brides sometimes cut their bouquet's ribbons into pieces and handed them out to attendants and friends as wedding souvenirs.

During both world wars, wedding bouquets tended to be simple nosegays, but in the twenties and thirties many brides carried sleek arm bouquets featuring one type of flower. Although calla lilies topped the list of popular blooms, Constance Spry fondly remembered one bouquet of white magnolia: "Three or four sprays only were used, but they were all well flowered and perfect in shape. They were arranged in a long slim sheaf, and the line of the chalices and brown stems against the white wedding gown was strikingly lovely." Another of her bouquets featured white camellias mounted on long wires bound with gold gauze. Held against an unusual gold wedding dress, the effect was enchanting.

After the Second World War, brides returned to carrying large round bouquets or floral-decorated prayer books (mine had a satin streamer decorated with two large purple-throated white orchids). Their flower-child daughters carried colorful masses or small bunches of garden blooms, wildflowers, and herbs. In the 1970s, small triangular structured bouquets that fell to a slender point were also popular. Then

A sheaf arrangement of white calla lilies provides a dramatic contrast to the understated wedding gown worn by a 1929 society bride.

in 1981, Lady Diana Spencer's lavish bouquet of white gardenias, orchids, freesia, stephanotis, and roses saw a return to the extravagant floral displays of the Edwardian era. Among Diana's lovely fall of white flowers were several golden Mountbatten roses in honor of Prince Charles's favorite uncle, Lord Louis Mountbatten, who had died in 1979.

Today, a bride is free to design a bouquet that expresses her own unique style and personality, from a small structured Victorian nosegay to loosely tied wildflowers or a sheaf of fragrant lilies reminiscent of the twenties. Colors — from massings of very pale ivories, champagnes, and glossy whites to explosions of brilliant jewel tones — are blended together with an artist's care to delight the eye. Sometimes a single unforgettable color or flower is showcased. Nor has Constance Spry's interest in texture or fragrance been forgotten: petals and foliage in various textures and shapes enhance any bridal bouquet, as does a spray of fragrant blooms.

CHOOSING THE FLOWERS

Sitting in a floral designer's shop surrounded by the fragrance and beauty of flowers cannot help but inspire a bride, even one who has only minimal knowledge of the florist's art.

A good place to start is with a favorite flower — a familiar one or perhaps an exotic variety that you have always dreamed of carrying at your wedding. A few blooms can be tucked into a bouquet, or the flower can provide a common design thread for the entire wedding. Roses, for example, could appear in the bridal bouquet and the attendants' bouquets, a tiny circlet of rosebuds could be worn by the flower girl, and the rose motif could be used on the china at the reception or in the fabric of the wedding dress or veil.

At the 1923 wedding of Lady Elizabeth Bowes-Lyon (now the Queen Mother), the bride carried a bouquet of white English roses and white Scottish heather, motifs that were also embroidered on her shoes. Customs from your own ethnic back-

Roses — either alone or mixed with other flowers — remain among the most popular blooms for a bridal bouquet. Here, delicate pink roses add a romantic note to a pastel bouquet of yellow and white orchids.

ground are a good source of inspiration — for example, traditional Spanish bouquets include orange blossoms while those from Ireland include lavender. Ask family friends and relatives or a floral designer for their suggestions on ways to honor your heritage in your bouquet.

Brides are no longer limited, as they once were, to a small number of seasonal flowers or expensive greenhouse blooms for their bouquets. Most flowers can now be purchased year-round, and new strains, colors, and varieties appear nearly every year. Your floral designer will be able to tell you if the flower you have chosen is appropriate for the type of wedding you are planning — for instance, whether it is delicate and will wilt easily at a summer outdoor wedding.

A favorite color or colors can also provide a floral design theme. White was used at the wedding of the Duke and Duchess of Windsor, while pink and white were featured at Consuelo Vanderbilt's. If your wedding is to be held close to a holiday, the colors associated with it may be used: soft mauves and purples for Easter or deep reds for Christmas. Be aware, though, that prices may be higher and florists are busiest during holidays and on Valentine's Day. (Quite by accident, my wedding date, December 27, turned out to be the most economical date of all. The church was already decorated with spectacular masses of dark red poinsettia plants supplied by the altar guild for Christmas!)

The next decision to make is the type of bouquet you would like to carry: a single-flower bouquet, such as Carolyn Bessette's small posy of lily of the valley; a mixed bouquet, such as Barbra Streisand's lovely gardenias and lily of the valley; or a single spray or bloom. Like

the wedding dress, the bridal bouquet should not be overwhelming or draw attention away from the bride. Large bouquets, like the one carried by Princess Diana, or the newly popular sheaf styles are appropriate for tall brides; small posies are more suitable for short brides. Round bouquets flatter every figure type and gown.

The style and color of your wedding dress should also be taken into consideration when choosing flowers: old-fashioned bouquets look best with Victorian- or Edwardian-style dresses, while contemporary bouquets suit modern designs. If you are choosing white flowers, roses, sweet peas, and ranunculus blend well with off-white dresses, while stephanotis, orchids, and hyacinths look marvelous against pure-white gowns.

FLOWERS FOR THE WEDDING PARTY

Constance Spry's favorite flowers for a bridesmaid's bouquet were pink camellias arranged in a Victorian posy with a fringe of their own leaves. Geraniums (*Pelargonium*) were another flower that she used in various shades of pink, cerise, and red. "These were massed into baskets for children to carry. Indeed this was the best way to use geraniums, for they would not have lasted if made into bouquets. We used many varieties, including some small-flowered scented geraniums, and the whole effect was unusual and good."

Every bride hopes her wedding party's flowers will produce a "good effect." Fortunately, there are many more options today than there used to be to make this possible. Bridesmaids' bouquets can be designed using different colors and flowers for each bridesmaid, while retaining the same shape and ribbons. Or the bouquets can pick up a flower or color from the bride's bouquet. Or each bridesmaid can carry one exquisite or unusual bloom. Limiting the design of the bridesmaids' bouquets to one color and one type of flower can save money without jeopardizing the

look of the bouquets. In fact, one-color and one-flower bouquets can look more impressive and expensive than mixed ones. Pretty baskets are still popular for flower girls, who may carry small blooms in them or rose petals to scatter in the path of the bride.

Corsages — pinned on a dress, attached to a purse, or worn on the wrist — are no longer the only floral options for the mothers and grandmothers of the bride and groom. At one recent wedding, the mothers carried small bouquets of sweet peas. As for boutonnieres, worn in the left lapel by the groom, fathers, grandfathers and groomsmen, they, too, can be striking tiny creations in the hands of a talented floral designer — although single rosebuds or a spray of lily of the valley never seem to go out of style. At his 1996 wedding to Carolyn Bessette, John Kennedy Jr. wore a single blue cornflower, his father's favorite bloom. Like the bride's bouquet, the groom's boutonniere tends to be different from those worn by the other men in the wedding party.

The fragrant white orange blossom, popularized by Queen Victoria on her wedding day,
is the inspiration for this charming groom's boutonniere created by acclaimed ribbon crafter Ellie Joos.

(Clockwise from top left)
A posy of ivory gerbera and purple
Monte Casino asters; a cascade
of white bouvardia, genista stems,
snowball viburnum, pink roses,
pink lisianthius, and trailing ivy;
a ribbon-tied posy of sweet peas;
a garden-inspired, hand-tied
pink bouquet of hydrangea,
Stargazer lilies, lisianthius,
roses and astilbe.

SETTING THE STAGE WITH FLOWERS

I fill very large and beautiful vases rather grandly with cut flowers,

placing these where they may be seen by the congregation and where they do

not hide from view the bride and groom.

— Constance Spry

FLOWERS, in spectacular or simple arrangements, have always played a major role in ceremony and reception decoration. At the 1963 wedding of Queen Elizabeth's cousin Princess Alexandra, huge urns were massed with spring flowers, while at Grace Kelly's wedding, the cathedral was decorated with large baskets of white lilac, her favorite flower. Less extravagant floral arrangements from the past have included Victorian posy bags — white triangular cloth pockets filled with blossoms and herbs and hung on pew ends — and simple pots of flowering spring bulbs or arrangements of autumn berries and fall leaves.

At the Victorian or Edwardian wedding breakfast, the table centerpieces tended to be large, elaborate, and full of greenery.

CHOOSING A FLORAL DESIGNER

*A*S ALWAYS, recommendations from friends or family members are helpful in choosing a designer. Before setting up an initial appointment to discuss ideas and budget (10 to 20 percent of your total budget should be set aside for flowers), you should know the date, time, and place for your ceremony and reception, and whether the wedding will be informal or formal. You should also be prepared to provide the designer with photographs of your dress and the bridesmaids' dresses, and, if possible, swatches of material. Showing the designer pictures from magazines or books of bouquets or arrangements you particularly like is useful, too.

Look at the designer's work in the shop and ask to see photographs of weddings he or she has done in the past. If you like what you see, the next step is to find out the answers to the following questions:

❧ Will the designer provide a written estimate for each item?

❧ How much is the deposit? (20 to 40 percent is standard)

❧ When is the final payment due?

❧ Will the shop transport the flowers to home, ceremony, and reception? Is there a fee for this?

❧ When will the flowers be delivered?

❧ Does the shop carry rental items such as urns?

❧ Is the designer familiar with your ceremony and reception sites?

Practical considerations for you to discuss with your designer include: the cost of a throwing bouquet, if you want to keep your flowers; how to prevent the bouquet from damaging your dress; and preservation techniques if you want to preserve your bouquet (freeze-drying is the best technique, although the process often costs double or triple the cost of the fresh bouquet).

FLORAL CHECKLIST

❧ Flowers to send to friends hosting dinners or other events in honor of the bridal couple

❧ Flowers to greet out-of-town bridal attendants in their hotel rooms

❧ Flowers sent as a gracious gesture to the groom's parents or grandparents

❧ The bridal bouquet

❧ The bridesmaids' bouquets

❧ The flower girl's bouquet or basket of rose petals

❧ Boutonnieres

❧ Small posies or corsages for the mothers and grandmothers of the bride and groom

❧ Flowers for the ceremony

❧ Flowers for the reception

❧ Flowers for older relatives or very close friends who are ill and unable to attend the ceremony. A card from the couple should accompany these flowers, saying they are "part of our wedding flowers that we wanted to share with you."

By the 1930s, they were much simpler, and today, in addition to traditional floral arrangements, the centerpiece may be a silver bowl of fruit, a collection of small potted plants serving double duty as favors, or several tiny vases, each holding a single flower. At the end of the reception, remember to arrange for the centerpieces to be given to grandmothers, mothers, favorite aunts, or older family friends, and for the reception flowers to be donated to a hospital or home for the aged.

If your wedding is being held at home, the flowers can be planned around what will be in bloom in the garden at that time. Barbra Streisand, whose lavish 1998 wedding to James Brolin was held at her Malibu estate, made a point of matching the colors of the floral arrangements inside the house with the flowers in her garden to create a visual flow from the interior to the exterior. A pretty wreath hanging on a gate or front door and flowers floating in a pool are other ways to welcome guests and to incorporate flowers in your wedding celebration.

Something Borrowed

You may not be able to hold your wedding in a French château, as the Windsors did,
but heritage homes and elegant old hotels can also provide romantic settings.

Cecil Beaton's photographs of Wallis taken shortly before her wedding are in many ways
more beautiful than the ones taken of her in her wedding outfit. Such photos are often more relaxed
portraits of the bride and provide a nice counterpoint to the formal wedding shots.

If your pets are members of the family, as the Duke and Duchess of Windsor's dogs were,
consider including them in a few candid wedding photos taken at home before the ceremony.

Masses of all-white flowers, like those Constance Spry arranged, can be
stunning in tall urns at the ceremony or reception.

Spry set her large floral arrangements on columns to make them look even more spectacular.

Wallis's choice of a simple dress and jacket, accessorized with stunning jewelry,
is always appropriate apparel for a repeat wedding. An elegant suit works just as well.
Matching gloves are an especially stylish touch.

In creating a cocktail for his bride, the Duke of Windsor gave Wallis something truly
original on their wedding day. Something equally original can be created by the groom for the bride,
the bride for the groom, or by the couple for their guests.

CHAPTER FOUR

POMP AND CIRCUMSTANCE

On the evening before the wedding . . . she came up to her room, singing.

There was a lovely feeling in the palace that night. We were all of us happy because

she was happy, and things had at last gone right for her.

— Marion Crawford, governess to Princess Elizabeth

PRINCESS ELIZABETH first met Prince Philip of Greece, a distant cousin, on a July day in 1939 when he was a dashing eighteen-year-old naval cadet and she was a thirteen-year-old schoolgirl. As Philip showed off on the tennis courts, devoured several platefuls of shrimp at teatime, and later energetically rowed a boat in the wake of the royal yacht, Elizabeth never took her eyes off him. For the shy princess, it was love at first sight.

Five years later, as the Second World War was drawing to a close, Elizabeth's attraction to Philip could no longer be dismissed as puppy love. They had been writing to each other on a regular basis, and after the annual Christmas pantomime performed by the Royal Family at Windsor Castle for their friends and relatives, Elizabeth's governess, Marion Crawford, remarked, "I have never known Lilibet more animated. There was a sparkle about her none of us had ever seen before." The reason for it was sitting in the front row — a smiling, obviously smitten Prince Philip.

Courtships, however, are a complicated business in royal families. In 1944, the year Elizabeth turned eighteen, Lord Louis Mountbatten and King George of Greece raised with Elizabeth's father the subject of Philip's possible marriage to her. Philip was not altogether pleased by their efforts and wrote Mountbatten, "Please, I beg of you, not too much advice in an affair of the heart. . . ." In any event, Elizabeth's father wrote back, "We both think she is too young for that now, as she has never met any young men of her own age." He liked Philip's intelligence and good humor but was obviously worried that Elizabeth's long seclusion at Windsor Castle during the war had prevented her from meeting other eligible young men. "Poor darlings," he wrote of Elizabeth and her fourteen-year-old sister, Margaret, on the day the war ended, "they have never had any fun yet."

To improve his daughters' social life, George VI began holding weekend parties in the country and giving private dances for them at Buckingham Palace. Elizabeth loved to dance and gleefully led conga lines snaking through the red-carpeted corridors and state apartments of the palace. Soon her name was linked with several young men from aristocratic families. But the only photograph displayed prominently on the mantelpiece of the Princess's sitting room was one of a bearded Philip in uniform.

By the summer of 1946, Elizabeth must have been tired of waiting — waiting to grow up, waiting for Philip to become a British subject. When Philip proposed to her directly, she ignored the advice of her parents and government advisers and accepted his proposal. At her father's request, however, their engagement remained a secret for nearly a year. Too many plans had already been made, including a tour of South Africa, to be eclipsed by the announcement of a royal betrothal. At parties that winter, the couple hid their feelings for each other and no one guessed. The photo of her dashing Prince remained on Elizabeth's mantelpiece, and

(Opposite) Princess Elizabeth's bridal gown of ivory duchess satin featured a tight-fitting bodice with heart-shaped neckline, and long tight sleeves. The flowing full skirt and the court train were embroidered with thousands of pearls and crystals in an intricate floral pattern.

tucked among Philip's clothes when he traveled was a small leather-framed photograph of his dark-haired princess — the only outward signs of their love.

Finally, on July 10, 1947, the King and Queen announced the "betrothal of their dearly beloved daughter," to the great delight of a war-weary country. As author Rebecca West wrote at the time, "It might have been folly to have a Royal Wedding in winter, but it was wise enough. People are tired of sadness, they need a party; they are tired of hate, they need to think of love; they are tired of evil, they need to think of goodness." The palace swung into high gear to plan the royal wedding of the decade, the first one to be broadcast around the world on radio.

Norman Hartnell, the royal dressmaker, was asked to design the wedding dress as well as the brides-maids' gowns. Royal weddings are solemn religious occasions, and the wedding gown must match the splendid surroundings. Hartnell's fairy-tale-princess gown was truly magnificent. Thousands of seed pearls and crystals had been embroidered by hand in intricate patterns of orange blossoms, star flowers, and white Tudor roses over the full skirt and fifteen-foot court train of transparent ivory silk tulle. Hartnell's inspiration for the long-sleeved dress was a Botticelli painting, of *Primavera*, which was in turn inspired by the classical goddess of flowers, Flora. In seven weeks, three hundred women finished the exquisite dress, which was delivered the night before the wedding.

On November 20, 1947, Elizabeth woke to the familiar sound of the Buckingham Palace pipers. At nine o'clock, Hartnell's assistants arrived and the familiar wedding flurry of activity began,

(Opposite) The bridal coach sweeps past the iron gates of Buckingham Palace on its way to Westminster Abbey. (Above) As the King stands ready to take his daughter's hand, Elizabeth pauses for a moment before entering the Abbey.

starting with the hour-long process of dressing the bride. At the last moment, Elizabeth realized her parents' gift of a double strand of pearls, which she planned to wear that day, were still with the other wedding presents at St. James's Palace. Her new private secretary was sent dashing through the crowds outside Buckingham Palace to retrieve them. As the necklace was being picked up, her grandmother's diamond-and-pearl tiara was set on Elizabeth's head — and promptly snapped in two. Fortunately, royal homes, unlike most commoners' houses, are well prepared for every emergency, and the old tiara was quickly repaired. The final scare of the morning — proving that even a royal wedding can have its panicky moments — saw courtiers frantically searching for the bride's orchid bouquet, which was eventually found in a cupboard.

At 11:16, with pearls on, tiara intact, and orchid bouquet in hand, Princess Elizabeth set off for Westminster Abbey with her father, to the thunderous cheers of the crowds of onlookers. Prince Philip, who had been given the title Duke of Edinburgh the evening before the wedding, waited patiently in the Abbey for the arrival of his bride. Amid a thrilling fanfare of trumpets, Elizabeth entered on her proud father's arm and began her walk up the long crimson-carpeted aisle, her diaphanous veil and train fanning out behind her. She was followed by two young pages dressed in kilts and eight bridesmaids in ivory dresses with wreaths of white flowers in their hair. At the altar, the King took his daughter's hand and placed it in the Archbishop's. Deeply touched, the King later remarked, "It is a far more moving thing to give your daughter away than to be married yourself."

(Above) With Elizabeth's left hand resting lightly on her father's arm,
the bridal procession begins the long walk up the crimson-carpeted center aisle. (Opposite)
The Archbishop of Canterbury, arrayed in his full white
and gold robes of State, conducts the marriage service as the royal pair
stand just below him on the sacrarium steps.
The King stands on his daughter's left.

Like every wedding ceremony, this one had been practiced the night before at a rehearsal. Everything went like clockwork until the two five-year-old pages carrying the long train were unable to unfasten it when it snagged on a tall candlestick. Much to their relief, the King himself helped them free it. One of the pages then tripped and nearly fell down on the way to sign the register. But such incidents lend a wonderfully human touch to any ceremony and should not be cause for worry.

After a wedding breakfast for one hundred and fifty guests in the palace ballroom, Elizabeth and Philip left in an open carriage, amid a shower of paper rose petals, to meet the train that would take them to their honeymoon retreat in the country. It was a chilly afternoon, and hotwater bottles had been tucked among the blankets to warm the couple and their one traveling companion — the bride's favorite corgi, Susan. It was a cozy, happy ending to a day full of pomp and splendor.

(Above) The happy couple waves from the balcony of Buckingham Palace. To the left stand bridesmaids Princess Margaret and Lady Cambridge. (Right) The formal portrait of the wedding party, taken in the Throne Room of the palace.

THE CEREMONY

Notwithstanding its splendour and national significance, the service

in this abbey is, in all essentials, exactly the same as it would be for any cottager who might

be married this afternoon in some small country church in a remote village in the Dales.

The same vows are taken; the same prayers offered; and the same blessings given.

— Dr. Cyril Garbett, the Archbishop of York

AT ELIZABETH AND PHILIP'S CEREMONY, the Queen Mother no doubt thought about her own wedding in the Abbey nearly twenty-five years before. Governess Marion Crawford, who sat nearby, wrote, "The past must have gone through her mind, as it went through mine, in a series of pictures of what had been an unusually happy family circle." Like every wedding ceremony, great pride and joy were mixed with a tinge of nostalgia.

The ceremony forms the emotional centerpiece of the wedding day. All the participants are swept up in the joyous event, beginning with their arrival at the ceremony. The ushers escort the women guests to their seats and generally oversee the seating of all the guests for the service. It is the best man's responsibility to brief the ushers before the wedding day on the guest list and any special seating arrangements. The front pews or chairs — those on the left for the bride's family, and those on the right for the groom's (the opposite, in Jewish ceremonies) — are usually decorated with special flowers and ribbons to mark them as family seats.

An usher greets the guest, asks for the guest's name if there is special seating, and offers his arm to a woman guest; a male companion or child follows behind. At a ceremony where the bride or groom has an unequal number of guests, the ushers should distribute the guests evenly on each side of the aisle.

About five minutes before the bride's entrance, in a Christian ceremony, an usher escorts the groom's mother to the front right pew. Her husband and family follow her, her husband sitting on her left in the pew. Shortly afterward, the head usher escorts the mother of the bride to the front left pew, where she leaves a vacant seat on the aisle for the bride's father. The music ceases and everyone waits in anticipation for the bridal procession to begin.

THE PROCESSIONAL

After the clergyman, the groom, and the best man enter from the side of the church, they take their places at the altar and face the door where the bridal procession will enter. The processional music begins, and the ushers march two by two up the aisle to take their places on the right-hand side of the altar, next to the groom and the best man. The bridesmaids follow in pairs. Next come the junior bridesmaid, the maid or matron of honor, the ring bearer or pages, and the flower girl. They form a row, or a grouping suggested by the clergyman at the rehearsal, on the left side of the altar.

GIVING THE BRIDE AWAY

After Princess Elizabeth's wedding, King George wrote to his daughter, saying, "I was so proud of you and thrilled at having you so close to me on our long walk in Westminster Abbey, but when I handed your hand to the Archbishop, I felt I had lost something very

(Opposite) An usher, holding programs and sprigs of rosemary, awaits the arrival of the wedding guests.
Rosemary, known as the herb of love, symbolizes fidelity.

precious. . . ." For any parent, the ritual of giving a daughter away, which is her family's acknowledgment of the new life she is about to begin, is an emotional moment. This part of the ceremony varies according to religious tradition.

In a traditional Catholic ceremony, once the father and daughter reach the altar, he removes her left arm from his right as she reaches out her right hand to her groom. He then takes his seat in the front pew next to his wife. However, this can be varied. For example, a father could lift his daughter's veil upon reaching the altar, kiss her good-bye, and place her right hand in the groom's left. Your priest will advise you on your options.

In most Protestant ceremonies, once the bride and her father reach the front of the church and stand beside the groom, the officiant asks some form of the question, "Who gives this woman in matrimony?" The father answers, "I do" or "Her mother and I do," and puts the bride's right hand in the clergyman's. If he chooses, he may give his daughter a kiss before joining his wife in the front right pew. The bride's mother sometimes joins the bride and her father at the altar and replies, "We do," with her husband, in answer to the officiant's question.

The bride may also be escorted up the aisle by a brother, relative, or close friend, or she may choose to walk up the aisle alone. In many Jewish ceremonies, both parents escort their daughter up the aisle of the synagogue and both parents give her away.

THE EXCHANGE OF RINGS

Princess Elizabeth's wedding ring was a plain band of Welsh gold fashioned from the same nugget used for her mother's wedding ring. Lord Milford Haven, the Duke of Edinburgh's best man, held on to it during the first part of the ceremony before giving the ring to the groom. The royal couple did not have a ring bearer and did not exchange rings.

Double-ring ceremonies only became popular after the Second World War. In a double-ring ceremony, when a ring bearer isn't used, the best man keeps the bride's wedding ring in a pocket until it is needed, while the maid or matron of honor wears the groom's ring on one of her fingers. When a ring bearer carries a pillow bearing the rings, the best man unties the ribbons holding the rings. He puts the bride's ring in a pocket and gives the groom's band to the maid or matron of honor for safekeeping.

PROMISES TO KEEP

As the Archbishop of York reminded the world during his broadcast address at Elizabeth and Philip's wedding ceremony, the royal service and vows do not differ from the standard Church of England

(Above) This charming ring bearer's pillow is made of two lace-trimmed handkerchiefs artfully stitched together and arrayed with ribbons and satin roses.

REHEARSAL ETIQUETTE

One or two nights before the ceremony in a place of worship, a rehearsal is scheduled with the officiant so that everyone in the wedding party knows what to do on the actual day of the wedding. The organist, musician, or a member of the musical group scheduled to play at the wedding should be present to learn when the music should be played. After the rehearsal, a party is hosted by the groom's parents, a relative, or a good friend of the couple. Invitations to the rehearsal dinner are sent to members of the wedding party, close relatives of the bride and groom, and out-of-town friends who are attending the festivities. The party, which should be a fun-filled, relaxing evening, can be anything from a black-tie dinner in a hotel to a picnic on the beach.

ritual. However, some royal couples have added their own touches to the ceremony. Princess Margaret, in her 1960 marriage to Antony Armstrong-Jones, included an ancient ritual — the binding of hands during the blessing of the ring — and the bride and groom also held hands as they exchanged their vows.

Well in advance of the ceremony, you should discuss with your officiant the vows, choice of prayers, and any special wording that you would like to include. Some religions are very strict about the marriage vows; others allow great freedom in what is said or not said at the service. For those brave couples who are not intimidated by speaking in public, memorizing your vows rather than repeating them after the clergyman can make this intensely personal moment even more meaningful.

Marriage officiants who are licensed to perform weddings in homes, hotels, or other places usually provide a selection of ceremonies and vows, which can be customized to suit your needs. For a civil ceremony at city hall, there are usually two services offered: a traditional religious service and a non-denominational one.

If you are writing your own vows, it is a good idea to keep them simple, short, and heartfelt. For inspiration, you might consult the many wedding anthologies now available. I remember a friend who had prepared beautiful vows but twice during the ceremony forgot what was to come next. Her groom, who knew how nervous she was in front of a crowd, had memorized her vows as well as his own and quietly whispered the lines to her. In that moment we all decided she had married a wonderful man.

THE RECESSIONAL

One of the most touching moments at Princess Elizabeth's wedding occurred during the recessional. As the couple approached the King and Queen, Elizabeth paused and curtsied deeply while Philip bowed.

For the recessional, the positions in the processional are reversed. The bride takes her groom's right arm and they walk first, sometimes stopping to kiss their parents before continuing down the aisle. They are followed by the maid or matron of honor with the best man, the ring bearer and flower girl, the junior bridesmaid, and the bridesmaids — each paired with an usher. (If there aren't enough ushers, the bridesmaids walk out two by two.)

Whether your ceremony takes place in a house of worship or in a public space such as an art gallery (above), be sure to discuss the vows, choice of prayers, and music with the officiant well in advance.

87

WEDDING MUSIC

The notes of Parry's Bridal March died away, the high,
stirring silver notes of a fanfare played by the trumpeters of the
Royal School of Music filled the morning air with gladness,
proclaiming that the bride had arrived.

— Louis Wulff, *Queen of Tomorrow*

WHILE THE GUESTS waited expectantly for Princess Elizabeth, they listened to Elgar's *Sonata in G major*, Widor's *Andante Cantabile*, Bach's "Fugue Alla Giga" and "Jesu, Joy of Man's Desiring," and Handel's *Water Music*. A fanfare of trumpets proclaimed the bride's arrival, followed by the choir singing the hymn, "Praise, My Soul, the King of Heaven," which had also been sung at the wedding of Elizabeth's parents. Gibbons's "Amen" brought the service to an end. During the signing of the register, Wesley's "Blessed Be the God and Father" was sung, and the recessional music was Mendelssohn's "Wedding March."

Just as Princess Elizabeth chose the music for her wedding ceremony, Prince Charles picked most of the selections for his 1981 wedding to Lady Diana Spencer. The processional music was Jeremiah Clarke's "Trumpet Voluntary," opera singer Kiri Te Kanawa sang an aria from Handel's *Samson* during the signing of the register, and the recessional music was Sir Edward Elgar's "Pomp and Circumstance March no. 4." Another Elgar piece — this time, the "Triumphal March" from *Caractacus* — was used for the recessional at Prince Andrew's 1986 wedding to Sarah Ferguson.

At the wedding of Prince Edward and Sophie Rhys-Jones in 1999, the "Marche Heroique" by Sir Herbert Brewer was played during the bride's procession to the altar, followed by the hymn "Ye Holy Angels Bright." After the ceremony, "Love Divine, All Loves Excelling" was sung, followed by "Where There Is Charity and Love, There Is God," and the royal favorite, "Let All the World in Every Corner Sing." As the register was signed, the choir sang Elgar's "Spirit of the Lord Is Upon Me" and Handel's "Amen Chorus." The music played for the recessional was the "Toccata" from Widor's *Fifth Symphony* and Sir William Walton's "Coronation March."

A wedding is set to music, and choosing the right selections — from the opening processional hymn to the last romantic dance before the guests depart — will ensure there isn't a single jarring note on this most important day.

A BRIDAL SONG

WORDS BY MARK LEMON.

MUSIC BY FRAN

Allegretto con espressione.

MUSIC FOR THE CEREMONY

PRELUDE

The Four Seasons ("Spring" or "Autumn") by Vivaldi
Concerto Grosso in D, Op. 3, no. 6 ("Vivace") by Handel
"Serenade" from *String Quartet*, Op. 3, no. 5 by Haydn
Orchestral Suite no. 3 in D ("Air") by Bach

PROCESSIONAL

Canon in D by Pachelbel
Water Music, Suite no. 1 in F ("Air") by Handel
The Four Seasons ("Winter") by Vivaldi
"Jesu, Joy of Man's Desiring" by Bach
Guitar Concerto in D, RV93 ("Largo") by Vivaldi
"Sinfonia" from *Cantata no. 156* by Bach

BRIDE'S MUSIC

"Bridal Chorus" from *Lohengrin* by Wagner
"Trumpet Voluntary" by Jeremiah Clarke
"Wedding March" from *The Marriage of Figaro* by Mozart
"Ave Maria" by Schubert
Trumpet Tune and Air in D by Purcell

INTERLUDE

"Arioso" by Bach
"Minuet" from *Berenice* by Handel
"Let the Bright Seraphim" by Handel
"Clair de Lune" by Debussy

RECESSIONAL

"Wedding March" from *Midsummer Night's Dream*
by Mendelssohn
"Minuet in F" from *Music for the Royal Fireworks* by Handel
"Ode to Joy" from the *Symphony no. 9* by Beethoven
Allegro movements from the trio sonatas
of Telemann, Mozart, or Handel
Brandenburg Concerto no. 1 ("Allegro") by Bach

The bride and groom should consider carefully the music for the ceremony. Some houses of worship do not allow non-religious music to be played; others are more flexible. Regardless of where the ceremony is held, the music should be memorable, familiar, and dignified, in keeping with the solemnity of the occasion. An organist, classical trio, string quartet, harpist, soloist, or choir are all possibilities, although recorded music can work well, too.

Many music stores have a nuptial section, where you can buy CDs of wedding music. The following suggestions (see box, left) from my old friend Peter Duchin, who has played at many weddings — and more White House parties than anyone else other than the Marine Corps Band! — are very appropriate.

MUSIC FOR THE RECEPTION

Today, when so many different types of music are popular, it can be a daunting task to choose music for the reception. Couples who are able to afford the considerable expense hire a classical trio to play at the ceremony, a jazz combo to perform during the cocktail hour, and a swing band for dancing. A good band, however, should be able to play a wide selection of music to cover all tastes — from your favorites to your parents' favorites. An experienced disc jockey can do the same. He or she should be able to accommodate your requests and make suggestions as well. Peter Duchin and his orchestra, for example, like to open with "Isn't It Romantic?" by Rodgers and Hart to put everyone in the mood. (Peter even taught it to the country music band that played at his daughter's 1997 wedding in Montana!)

Before asking a band to play at your reception, it's always wise to see a live performance, rather than relying on videos or tapes. Some bands will ask permission for you to visit another couple's reception for a short time to hear them play. You may also be asked to return the favor for another client. Once you have decided on a band, you should negotiate a contract with them. The written agreement should include the date and time of the reception, the address of the reception site, a contact name and telephone number, the name of the bandleader, the number and type of instruments, the number of hours the band will play, the frequency and length of breaks, the name of the person authorized to request overtime (the best man, for example), a breakdown of costs (including overtime rates), what the musicians will wear, whether the bandleader will act as emcee, and the setup and cleanup time.

Every bride would love to be able to write to her orchestra leader after her wedding, as television producer Susan Fales-Hill did to Peter Duchin, "You played with a love and passion that turned our wedding into a celebration of friendship and love." And every groom would like to echo Arnold Schwarzenegger's thanks, "You played the first waltz slow enough so I didn't fall all over Maria [the bride] and Eunice [her mother]!" The key is finding a band that has played at many wedding receptions, that has a wide repertoire, and that is led by a musician who can transform a reception into a wonderful party for young and old alike.

Music creates mood, and nowhere is the mood of a wedding more relaxed than at the reception. Remember to select the music — and the musical accompaniment — that best suits the style and setting of your reception and the ages of your guests.

WEDDING VEILS AND HEADPIECES

The bride sometimes wears her veil over her face

as she goes up the aisle but, returning, it is thrown back,

showing her happy face to the world.

— Mrs. Burton Kingsland, *Etiquette for All Occasions*, 1901

IN VICTORIA'S TIME, wedding veils were considered symbols of purity, to be worn only once by a bride and then passed down to her daughters. A borrowed veil of handmade lace was considered to be very lucky. Although Victoria's lace veil was criticized by some ladies of fashion as being too short, it was worn and cherished by three of her descendants. Princess Elizabeth departed from this royal tradition by wearing a tulle veil.

If you have inherited an heirloom veil and would like to wear it on your wedding day, bring it with you when you select your dress. To look spectacular, the style of a heritage veil, as well as its color, should complement the gown. An elaborate flow of lace looks best with a simple gown; an aged ivory veil blends well with a wedding dress fabric of a similar hue. The weight of a lace veil often requires an upswept hairstyle or a hairpiece to lift it from the face and to help the bride cope with it as she proceeds up the aisle.

Today's gossamer creations are most often made entirely of tulle, which is admired for its romantic, ethereal effect. They are designed in numerous lengths (see page 96), and are choosen to suit the style of the bride, the dress she will wear, and the formality of the wedding.

Sometimes several veils of various lengths are worn together. If your dress has beautiful details on the back, such as a row of buttons or silk flowers, you may prefer a very sheer veil so that these decorations don't disappear altogether. As in all wedding apparel, the key is to strive for simplicity. What you don't want to hear as you float up the aisle is your guests whispering, "Is she in there somewhere?"

(Above) In this magical photograph, the star flowers on Princess Elizabeth's diaphanous veil seem to float in the air as her attendants adjust the veil and train before the bride's entrance into Westminster Abbey.

VEIL STYLES

❦ FLYAWAY. This veil falls in multiple layers to the shoulder. It is suitable for informal and semiformal weddings.

❦ ELBOW LENGTH. Just touching the elbow, this veil may be made from a single, double, or triple layer of tulle. Although appropriate for most weddings, it is usually paired with a longer veil for formal ceremonies.

❦ FINGERTIP. Suitable for all but the most formal weddings, this veil reaches the wrists or fingertips.

❦ WALTZ. Extending nearly to the floor, the waltz veil is best suited to a semiformal wedding.

❦ CHAPEL. This seven- to eight-foot veil is the most popular style for a formal wedding.

❦ CATHEDRAL. A cathedral veil, which is longer than nine feet, is reserved for very formal wedding ceremonies held in a large church or cathedral.

❦ MANTILLA. Made in a variety of lengths, this veil is trimmed with a wide border of lace.

❦ WATERFALL. This veil cascades from the crown of the head, creating a waterfall effect. It may have a single, double, or triple layer of tulle and is available in various lengths.

❦ SHAWL. The ideal choice for a strapless gown, this veil covers the shoulders and looks like a shawl in the front and a long, soft veil in the back. It looks best in a chapel length.

❦ BLUSHER. A blusher is the part of a veil that covers the face. It comes in various lengths, from shoulder to elbow length, and is often detachable.

(From left to right) Elbow Length, Chapel, Mantilla, and Shawl Veils.

Headpieces anchor the romantic cloud of veil. They should complement the wedding dress and, if made of fabric — as the Juliet cap and circular headband are — should match it in color. Wearing a bridal wreath of flowers is a tradition that dates back to the Middle Ages. At Sarah Ferguson's 1986 wedding to Prince Andrew, the bride wore a wreath of roses as she walked up the aisle but exchanged it, before the recessional, for a tiara denoting her new status as the Duchess of York. Some brides dispense with a headpiece and veil altogether and wear a few well-chosen flowers, an ornate pin, or an antique comb in their hair.

Brides planning a formal ceremony may consider wearing a blusher with their veil. This light, single layer of tulle, worn during the processional, is usually lifted off the face by a family member before the ceremony begins — as Christopher Rhys-Jones did just before his daughter Sophie joined Prince Edward at the altar. If you opt to follow the age-old tradition of wearing a blusher during the ceremony, be sure the veil sits away from your face so as not to interfere with the recital of your vows. Your groom (or maid or matron of honor, if the groom forgets) will then lift the veil after you are pronounced husband and wife. Often, everyone forgets, and the bride has to lift the veil for the much-anticipated first kiss!

Many blushers today are detachable and are removed after the ceremony. The rest of the veil is usually removed at the reception after the first dance.

TIARAS AND HAIR ORNAMENTS

Like trains, glittering tiaras say "princess" to every little girl at heart. When choosing from the wide variety that is available — from silver tiaras incorporating Celtic knots and symbols to small rhinestone tiara combs — keep in mind the style of your dress and the other jewelry you may wish to wear. You want to avoid looking like a pageant queen or a fairy godmother. A very simple necklace (or no necklace at all) and a pair of pearl or dia-

mond stud earrings are usually the best accessories to wear with a tiara. Tiaras can be worn with or without a veil and work with any hairstyle, long or short.

Sparkling hair ornaments can take the place of a tiara or a headpiece and veil. A bride should make sure that all the jewelry she is wearing matches. A simple pearl necklace or a diamond necklace with matching earrings are always suitable.

Princess Elizabeth's ethereal tulle veil was held in place by a tiara of diamonds and pearls, which blended beautifully with the magnificent patterning of crystals and pearls embroidered on her gown and court train.

Something Borrowed

Repeating a detail from the wedding gown on the bridesmaids' dresses
can be a charming and unifying touch. The appliquéd blossoms and pearls on the skirts of her
attendants' gowns echoed those on Princess Elizabeth's train.

Cut-glass and pearl beads, like the thousands
on Elizabeth's dress, add a magical shimmer to a gown, particularly in soft candlelight.

"Praise, My Soul, the King of Heaven," the introductory hymn
sung by the choir at Princess Elizabeth's wedding, was one of her favorites. It had also been
sung at her parents' wedding, which added another touch of tradition to the ceremony.
Be sure to ask your mother and grandmothers about their weddings.

Elizabeth and Philip's favorite pastimes — including cricket,
horseback riding and swimming — were depicted on sugar plaques that decorated
their elaborate four-tiered wedding cake. You might consider cake
decorations that reflect your own interests.

Before embarking on her new life with Philip,
Princess Elizabeth took the time to write a thank-you letter to her mother.
Writing a letter or even e-mailing your parents to thank them for their help and
advice over the years is a thoughtful, reassuring gesture.

The processional route for the royal wedding was lined
with banners decorated with the couple's entwined initials. A small, monogrammed banner
(vertical, not horizontal) hanging outside the reception venue lends a festive note.
A flag or banner company can custom-make one for you.

Elizabeth always wore a thin platinum bracelet that contained one of the
smallest watches in the world — and she wore this favorite piece of jewelry at her wedding, too.
If you're attached to a certain ring, necklace, or bracelet, keep it in mind
when you choose your wedding dress and accessories.

ROYAL WEDDINGS

The Duke & Duchess of York

(Below) On April 26, 1923, Lady Elizabeth Bowes-Lyon (now the much adored Queen Mother) married Prince Albert, the Duke of York and second son of the English king. Her wedding ring was the first to be fashioned from the single nugget of Welsh gold that has since been used for several other royal rings, including Queen Elizabeth's and Princess Diana's.

1863   1923

The Prince of Wales & Princess Alexandra of Denmark

(Above) Following the fashion introduced by her mother-in-law, Queen Victoria, Alexandra wore a wreath of orange blossoms and a white gown trimmed with Honiton lace at her 1863 wedding at St. George's Chapel, Windsor Castle.

Sophie Rhys-Jones & Prince Edward

(Below) England's most recent newlyweds also chose St. George's Chapel for their wedding on June 19, 1999.

Princess Anne & Lieutenant Mark Phillips

(Below right) Anne's nine-year-old brother, Prince Edward, and her nine-year-old cousin, Lady Sarah Armstrong-Jones, were the only attendants at the princess's understated November wedding at Westminster Abbey.

Sarah Ferguson & Prince Andrew

(Far right) The newly titled Duchess of York waves to jubilant crowds outside Westminster Abbey. (Above) A commemorative fan from the July wedding.

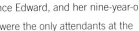

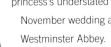

1973   1986

King Carl Gustaf of Sweden

(Below) Like the final scene from a "happily-ever-after" fairytale, the King marries the lovely commoner — a German translator, Silvia Sommerlath — he met four years earlier at the Munich Olympic Games.

1976

1933

Princess Caroline of Monaco

(Below left) Caroline's marriage to Prince Ernst August of Hanover, an old family friend, on January 23, 1999, promises the happiness that has eluded the eldest daughter of Princess Grace for so long. Caroline's first marriage, a ceremonial royal wedding to playboy Phillipe Junot on June 29, 1978, ended two years later. In 1990, her fairytale romance and marriage to Italian businessman Stefano Casiraghi (right) ended tragically when the boyish Casiraghi was killed in a speedboat-racing accident.

1978

1999

Heiress Weds Prince

(Above) Wealthy Woolworth heiress Barbara Hutton, who "collected" Hollywood leading men and pseudoroyalty, poses with one of her husbands, Prince Alexis Mdivani of Georgia, outside the Russian Orthodox Church in Paris.

Princess Mathilde d'Udekem d'Acoz

(Below) Crown Prince Philippe of Belgium and his young bride kiss after their civil wedding on December 4. The ceremony, which marked the last royal wedding of the twentieth century, was conducted in French, Dutch, and German — the country's three official languages.

1999

CHAPTER FIVE

A FRONT-PAGE WEDDING

They walked out together and I suggested they face each other

from a distance and hold hands looking into each other's eyes. A slight breeze

came up and blew the veil behind her. How did I know I was

photographing such people of destiny?

— Photographer Toni Frissell

ALTHOUGH none of their many friends imagined what an indelible impression Jacqueline Bouvier and John F. Kennedy would ultimately make on their country and the world, no one ever doubted their ability to succeed in any endeavor they undertook. Jackie's intelligence, classic good looks, and incredible sense of style marked her as a very special young woman, while the charismatic, boyishly handsome Jack Kennedy was a congressman who was obviously going places.

They were first introduced in May 1951 at the Washington home of mutual friends, Charlie and Martha Bartlett. After dinner, Jack walked his enchanting new acquaintance to her car and asked her out. Unfortunately, before Jackie could answer, a former boyfriend surprised them both by jumping up from the back seat of her black Mercury. The moment was spoiled, Jack said good-night, and the two didn't meet again until over a year later. During that time, Jack was busy running for the Senate, and Jackie began a job as the "inquiring photographer" for the *Washington Times-Herald*. This involved stopping well-known people on the street, asking them a question, and taking their picture.

The next time the two met was at another dinner party given by the Bartletts (whom Jackie later thanked for their "shameless match-making"). Although twelve years separated them in age, Jack and Jackie soon discovered they shared a great many interests: a love of reading and board games, quiet dinners and good conversation, and a love of the outdoors, particularly the sea. Both had spent memorable summers on the Atlantic seaboard — Jackie at Hammersmith Farm, her mother and stepfather's twenty-eight-room Newport mansion, and Jack at his parents' summer home in Hyannis Port on Cape Cod, where he and his eight siblings had indulged their passion for swimming, tennis, sailing, and touch football.

During this period of their romance, I remember being home

(Above) An obviously happy John Kennedy and Jacqueline Bouvier, two months before their wedding —
the first of many photographs of the famous couple to grace the cover of *Life* magazine. (Opposite) The formal bridal portrait.

from my embassy posting in Paris and having lunch with Jackie in Washington. We were both chatting about the French capital, where she had studied at the Sorbonne. Then at some point, she began talking about Jack Kennedy, and it became evident from the excitement in her eyes that this was someone she cared about very deeply. As for Jack, his political aide and friend Dave Powers remembers the country's most eligible bachelor saying in May 1953, "I have never met anyone like her — she's different from any girl I know. Do you want to see what she looks like?" He then pulled out some photographs, and Powers recalled that "the pictures showed two people clearly in love."

A month later, while Jackie was in England photographing the coronation of Queen Elizabeth, the now junior senator from Massachusetts proposed by cable, in typical John F. Kennedy style — short on sentiment and romance, long on urgency and efficiency. A few weeks later, their engagement was officially announced — sealed by a magnificent square-cut emerald-and-diamond ring that Jack had placed on his twenty-four-year-old fiancée's finger. With the wedding date set for September 12, the two mothers met to begin making plans, but both had very different ideas of the kind of celebration that should be held. While Rose Kennedy, at her husband Joe's insistence, wanted a large traditional Catholic wedding with extensive press coverage to further Jack's political career, Janet Auchincloss considered publicity vulgar and favored a small, private affair at Hammersmith Farm.

The Kennedys' wishes prevailed. More than seven hundred guests crowded into St. Mary's Church in Newport, Rhode Island, to watch the young couple exchange vows — and an additional

six hundred, including reporters, film celebrities, and politicians, received invitations to the reception. Unfortunately, I was in Rome working for Ambassador Luce and was unable to return home for the wedding. I was heartbroken I could not be there. From all accounts, the wedding was a thoroughly splashy, glamorous affair — Old World society, with a bit of New York café society, a sprinkling of Irish politicos from Boston, and some stuffy Newport names, all mixed together in a well-shaken social cocktail.

On the morning of the wedding, Jackie was helped into her gown by its designer, Ann Lowe, an African-American dressmaker who had created ball gowns for some of New York's wealthiest society women. Jackie had, of course, wanted a wedding dress by a top New York or Paris designer, but the Auchincloss budget for the wedding was already stretched to the limit. The gown, although not lavish, was beautifully worked — its taffeta skirt was embellished with large circles of interwoven bands of tucking and tiny wax orange blossoms, and its creamy ivory color matched her grandmother's heirloom rosepoint veil. As she slipped on the beautiful diamond bracelet Jack had given her the night before as a wedding gift, what must have weighed on her mind was the distressing news that her beloved father, the dashing "Black Jack" Bouvier, would not be giving her away.

In 1940, Jackie's parents had undergone a bitter divorce, brought about partly by Jack Bouvier's gambling, drinking, and philandering. Although her former husband had played father of the bride only five months previously at the wedding of Lee, their younger daughter, Janet Auchincloss was worried that Jack would

The elaborate Gothic structure of St. Mary's Church proved to be a fitting location for one of the most eagerly anticipated weddings of the year. More than seven hundred guests witnessed the solemn Catholic service presided over by Archbishop Cushing of Boston.

be in no shape to play a part in the society wedding the Auchinclosses were planning for Jackie. It was already being billed as "The Wedding of the Year." However, Jack Bouvier — who, for all his faults, was a loving father — was determined to be at his daughter's side. He attended the rehearsal without incident, but on the day of the wedding, the newspapers were told that he was too "ill" (perhaps a euphemism for "drunk") to attend.

It is a measure of Jackie's courage and sense of duty that she was able to overcome her personal disappointment and present a smiling, confident face to the world on her wedding day. She entered St. Mary's, which was decorated with pink gladioli and white chrysanthemums, on the arm of her stepfather. Without any sign of nerves, she walked up the aisle holding a large bouquet of pink and white spray orchids, stephanotis, and miniature gardenias, looking radiant in the glow of light that streamed through the stained-glass windows.

Even as a young bride, Jackie's gift for skillfully combining the old with the new was apparent. Ambassador and Mrs. Kennedy had given her a diamond pin in the shape of a leaf as a wedding present. She wore it on the bodice of her dress. Jack's diamond bracelet and the Kennedys' gift of jewelry represented her future with her new

family, while her grandmother's veil and a simple strand of family pearls were reminders of the past and her own heritage.

Jack smiled broadly as his bride joined him at the altar. As always, he was impeccably tailored, although a little the worse for wear. He had scratched his face the day before in one of the Kennedy family's favorite activities — a game of touch football. Archbishop Richard Cushing presided over the solemn forty-minute ceremony, and a special blessing sent by the Pope was read. St. Mary's was soon filled with the sound of the hymns "Ave Maria," "Panis Angelicus," and "Jesu, Amor Mi," beautifully sung by renowned tenor Luigi Vena. After the couple exchanged their wedding vows, Jackie returned down the aisle on the arm of an obviously happy and proud Jack Kennedy.

"The Couple of the Year" stepped out into the sunlight to hundreds of waiting cameras and the cheers of three thousand well-wishers. The noisy scene was a foretaste of their future lives together — fame, acclaim, and an aggravating lack of privacy. "It was extremely exciting for us in the wedding party," remembered bridesmaid Aileen Bowdoin Train. "This glamorous young senator and this beautiful girl. . . . Just masses of crowds outside craning and pushing and crowding in and shoving just to see the bride."

Outside the church, thousands of onlookers strain for a glimpse of the newlyweds as hordes of reporters and photographers capture the historic moment for the press. No one in the wedding party had anticipated the extent of the public's interest in the dashing senator from Massachusetts and his beautiful young bride.

I daresay Jackie must have got a little tired smiling and shaking hands, but I can't think of a more appropriate introduction to her new life as the wife of a political figure.

— Rose Kennedy

THE OUTDOOR WEDDING RECEPTION

*I*T TOOK MORE THAN two hours for all the guests at Jack and Jackie's wedding reception to go through the receiving line inside the Auchincloss mansion. After greeting the last of the well-wishers, the wedding party headed out onto the lush lawns and gardens of Hammersmith Farm, with its splendid view of Narragansett Bay — a magical location for an outdoor wedding reception.

Although the Kennedys were not yet ensconced at 1600 Pennsylvania Avenue when they married, the grounds of the White House also lend themselves beautifully to a wedding celebration. Eight presidential daughters and one president (Grover Cleveland, in 1886) have staged their weddings in the official residence, and the June 1971 marriage of President Richard Nixon's daughter Tricia to Edward Cox was the first wedding ceremony to be held outdoors at the White House. The couple exchanged vows in a small, white wrought-iron pavilion set up in the Rose Garden, which had been planted when Jacqueline Kennedy was First Lady. Every aspect of the wedding reflected the spring-garden theme — from the organdy-brimmed picture hats of the four bridal attendants to the profusion of lilacs, peonies, roses, and other spring flowers indoors and out.

Outdoor settings are suitable for both formal and informal ceremonies and receptions. Obviously, the White House gardens or

A radiant Jacqueline Kennedy adjusts her veil
as she sits down beside her new husband to enjoy fruit salad in hollowed-out
pineapple halves — the first course at their outdoor wedding luncheon.

The night sky, visible through the clear plastic ceiling of the tent, provides a perfect backdrop for the canopy of tiny lights that illuminates this magical wedding reception. The choice of a single color — white — for the floral arrangements and table settings enhances the romantic glow that fills every corner of the reception area. Elegant candelabra and bouquets of white roses stand high atop garlanded pillars, while votives, white linen and crystal sparkle at every table.

the grounds of a grand country house like Hammersmith Farm are not available to most brides, but more modest substitutes can be found with a bit of hunting. The formal gardens of a historic home, for example, offer a perfect setting for a Victorian- or Edwardian-style wedding reception — perhaps a formal tea held between three and five o'clock, with white linen tablecloths, pretty tea napkins trimmed with lace, and old-fashioned roses arranged in antique china bowls. Guests can enjoy delicious little sandwiches, fruit scones, fresh berries, elegant pastries, and, of course, champagne.

Historic buildings add a sense of occasion that modern hotels are hard-pressed to duplicate. A variety of sites, with a choice of architectural styles, is often available in or near large cities. Stately homes provide elegant period settings, as do wonderfully designed commercial buildings, museums, and art galleries. The administrators of historic sites can advise you on their regulations. Questions that need to be asked include: Can alcohol be served on the premises? Is the wiring capable of handling your electrical requirements? Are the rest rooms adequate for the number of guests you plan to invite? Are kitchen facilities available? Where can people park? For any outdoor wedding, contingency plans must be made in case of bad weather, but this is particularly true of historic homes where large areas of the interior may be out-of-bounds. Tents erected on the grounds are often a necessity in this case.

THE MAGIC OF TENTS

After all the hugs and handshakes of the receiving line had been given, Jack and Jackie headed for the dance floor set up under a large blue-and-white-striped tent. As they stepped onto the floor, the dancing stopped, every conversation ended, the champagne sipping ceased, and all eyes were on the attractive young couple. When Meyer Davis's orchestra began to play "I Married an Angel," Jack and Jackie took off in a more than adequate fox-trot (no waltzes for Jack!). Then Joe Kennedy, Jackie's new father-in-law, cut in, followed by a string of brothers-in-law, stepbrothers, and groomsmen, all wanting a turn on the dance floor with the newest member of the Kennedy family.

No outdoor wedding reception is complete without one or more tents. During the day, they add a touch of fantasy to any out-

door setting; at night, they capture the romantic glow of candlelight. Two basic types are available: a frame tent for non-grass areas like patios, and a pole tent that can be staked on grass. When considering the different styles and sizes, allow approximately one square yard per person plus additional space for waiters' stations, bars, and a dance floor. For an additional cost, some companies provide a draped fabric liner to cover the ceiling of the tent. You may also want to consider air conditioners or heaters, a wooden floor for dancing, and lighting (hundreds of tiny lights strung behind the fabric liner or from the center of the ceiling create a delightful, magical effect, and hanging crystal chandeliers are spectacular). Sometimes tent companies also rent tables, chairs, and other equipment.

Your floral designer can suggest ways to decorate the inside of the tent — from greenery or cascading flowers to cover the interior posts to a boxwood or flowered hedge around the dance floor.

OUTDOOR BUFFETS

As the guests at Jackie and Jack's wedding reception helped themselves to a luncheon buffet and stood or found places at small tables scattered about the grounds, the wedding party held the place of honor at a horseshoe-shaped table draped in crisp white linen edged with a garland of fresh flowers and greenery. Behind the head table, an ivy-covered wall provided a wonderfully textured natural backdrop for photographs.

The menu for the Kennedys' wedding luncheon, chosen by Janet Auchincloss, included fruit salad served in hollowed-out pineapple halves (a new presentation at the time), the proverbial creamed chicken (standard luncheon fare), and a dessert of ice cream molds in the shape of roses. Jackie as a bride showed an immediate interest in unusual, sophisticated food. Conventional menus, like the one for her wedding reception, never appeared at her own dinner parties.

Although sit-down lunches and dinners are always appropriate for an outdoor reception, buffets seem tailor-made for these events. The modern trend is station buffets, with separate tables for different types of food. Among the delicious possibilities are: raw bars featuring oysters, cooked shrimp, mussels, clams, and caviar; carving tables laden with roasts of beef, chicken, and lamb; and cold salad, barbecued food, cheese, pasta/risotto, or dessert stations.

AT THE RECEPTION

THE RECEIVING LINE

The bride's mother stands first in the line, then the groom's father, groom's mother, bride's father, bride, groom, maid or matron of honor, junior bridesmaid, and other bridesmaids in order of their age. Flower girls and ring bearers are too young to be included in the receiving line. Often only the father of the bride stands in line, and both fathers may cut in and out of the line, as may the bridesmaids after the first half hour. But the bride, groom, and their mothers should remain until the last guests have offered their congratulations.

At a wedding reception held in the home of the bride's father and stepmother, the stepmother would stand first in line — but at any other venue, only the bride's mother would stand in the receiving line. In the first case, an appropriate order would be stepmother, groom's mother, bride's mother, bride's father, bride, groom, and bride's attendants.

While waiting to be received, guests should be offered a drink and asked to sign the guest book. Members of the bridal party should not hold glasses of champagne while in the receiving line. However, discreet sips from glasses placed on a table behind the wedding party are just fine. Wedding guests should not be holding glasses when going through the receiving line either. With all the hugging and showing of one's joy, it's hard to hold a glass of champagne or anything else and not spill it.

WHO SITS WHERE?

At a formal sit-down wedding reception, place cards are included at every table; at an informal reception, they appear only at the bride's table. Single cards or "tent" cards are positioned in one of several places: above the forks at the upper left of the place setting; on top of a napkin set in the middle of the plate; leaning against the stem of a glass; or just above the middle of the plate. The guest's first and last names are written on the place card so that people passing by can recognize who is sitting where; it also enables each person to know who his or her dinner partners are.

At the parents' table, the groom's father sits to the right of the mother of the bride; the bride's father sits opposite, with the groom's mother on his right. The clergyman might sit on the left of the bride's mother; the bride's grandfather might sit on the other side of the groom's mother, and so on. Family members are alternated with distinguished guests or very close friends.

As guests arrive at a large reception, helpers with lists of guests (arranged alphabetically) and their assigned table numbers should inform guests where they are to sit. This can be done in

At the bride's table, the maid or matron of honor sits next to the groom, and the best man next to the bride. The bridesmaids and ushers take alternating places on either side of the best man and maid or matron of honor. When the wedding party is large, the spouses or dates of the attendants sit at their own table nearby; otherwise, it is nice to invite them to join the bridal table.

two ways: large seating charts can be posted on easels outside the room, showing where each guest sits at each numbered table; or each guest may be given a small table card with his or her table number written on it. Guests enter the room and find their places by looking for their table number. These numbers, often on tall stanchions, should be removed by the waiters in the middle of the second course.

Choosing seasonal foods ensures high quality and the best prices. Spring foods might include lamb, veal, and pork, asparagus, baby lettuces, fiddleheads, and morels. For summer, offer grilled foods, fish, tomatoes, new potatoes, berries, and peaches. Autumn suggests roasted meats, squash, corn, sweet peppers, wild mushrooms, figs, apples, and pears.

At the 1997 wedding reception for Vice President Al Gore's daughter, Karenna, which took place on the grounds surrounding the Vice President's white Victorian mansion, one of the bride's favorite dishes was served: minted lamb in tomato cups. Many couples today like to include on the menu foods they particularly enjoy. If you are planning a summer wedding, though, be sure that the food you choose will hold up well in warm weather.

When President Lyndon Johnson's daughter Lynda Bird married at the White House in 1967, guests feasted on the most elegant food of the period. Hot appetizers included crabmeat bouchées, stuffed mushrooms, miniature shish kebabs, quiche lorraine, and country ham with biscuits; cold platters featured smoked salmon with capers, iced shrimp, raw vegetables with dip, assorted cheeses, and finger sandwiches; and dessert choices of miniature éclairs, cream puffs, chocolate roulades, fruit tartlets, and petits-fours were offered.

Whether you choose the station approach or long traditional buffet tables, the food should be replenished often so that it remains fresh and attractive-looking. Wait staff should also be instructed to pick up used glasses, plates, and silverware as guests come and go. If long tables are used, they should be freestanding so that two lines of guests can be served simultaneously. If the guest list exceeds fifty people, plan to have at least two buffet tables. Unless your reception is a cocktail-style party where the majority of guests stand and talk, you might consider serving a first course or dessert at the dining tables so that your guests don't feel they are spending the entire meal standing in line.

Hammersmith Farm, with its expansive lawns and oceanfront view, was the perfect location for Jackie and Jack's wedding reception. The grounds could accommodate the twelve hundred guests invited to the luncheon — and the relaxed outdoor setting suited the informal nature of the Kennedy clan.

THE WEDDING TOASTS

Now, you're going to have to speak for the groom. I want you to be funny.

I want you to be clever.

— Joe Kennedy to guest George Smathers

ALTHOUGH wedding toasts are given at the wedding reception, the toasting tends to be the most spirited and memorable at the traditional rehearsal dinner hosted the night before the wedding by the groom's family. At the dinner given on the evening of September 11 by Ambassador and Mrs. Kennedy at Newport's exclusive Clambake Club, the toasting lasted for hours. Jack's ushers and groomsmen all possessed a great sense of humor, as did Jackie's bridesmaids, which made the competition for "the most amusing toast" very lively indeed.

Jackie proved she was up to the task as well. When her husband-to-be joked to the guests that because journalists were the bane of politicians, he was marrying Jackie to end her career as a member of the fourth estate, Jackie responded by saying that her fiancé, who had won the Pulitzer Prize for his book, *Profiles in Courage*, had written to her only once during their courtship. She held up a postcard from Bermuda and read it aloud: "Wish you were here. Jack."

One of the earliest recorded toasts was proposed by Rowena, the daughter of the Saxon king, Hengist, at her wedding feast in A.D. 450. She toasted her new husband, King Vortigern, with the phrase, "Long, King, be of health." The raising and touching of glasses after a toast also dates back to ancient times. It was believed that making a noise frightened away the evil spirits that entered a drinker's body along with the alcohol.

While Joe Kennedy believed a funny, clever toast was required at his son's wedding, toasts can be amusing, serious, teasing, or heartfelt. Most important, they should be well rehearsed and under three minutes in length (they can be somewhat longer at the rehearsal dinner).

The best man orchestrates who toasts first, second, third, and so on, at both the rehearsal dinner and the reception. This ensures that a certain protocol is observed — for example, the couple's parents should be allowed to speak before a loquacious old pal of the groom. In fact, one of the responsibilities of the best man is to cut off anyone who is boring and too drunk to notice it!

He begins by making the first toast, to the bride. Then he calls on: the groom to toast the bride (and possibly her parents); the bride to toast the groom (and perhaps both sets of parents); the father and/or mother of the bride to toast the couple; the father and/or mother of the groom to toast the couple; a grandparent or two is often called on; the siblings of the bride and groom come next; the maid or matron of honor, followed by ushers and bridesmaids who want to make toasts; and, finally, the friends of the bride and groom. The person being toasted does not drink at the end of the toast but remains seated, smiling at the person making the toast. After everyone else has sealed their toast with a sip of wine, he or she can follow suit.

(Above) Best man Robert Kennedy proposes a toast as Jackie exchanges a glance with her sister and matron of honor, Lee Bouvier Canfield.

(Above and opposite) Photographer Toni Frissell's skill
at capturing both the elegance and the ease of the Kennedy wedding
party is evident in these evocative outdoor images taken on the grounds
of Hammersmith Farm. (Left) In this informal photograph,
a gust of wind catches Jackie's heirloom lace veil.

PHOTOGRAPHY AND VIDEOGRAPHY

At a quarter to one, a big limousine drove into the portico.

It was a radiant Jackie and her handsome newlywed husband. When she saw me with

my camera, she said, "Toni is a good friend of mine. Let's give her a chance

to get a good picture before the guests arrive."

— Photographer Toni Frissell

*J*ACKIE'S thoughtfulness toward her friend Toni Frissell was a typical gesture on her part and also reflected her own experiences as a photojournalist. She had actually photographed a wedding herself earlier that year — on April 18, 1953, her sister, Lee, had married Michael Canfield. After catching the bouquet, Jackie had taken photographs of the ushers for her column.

Toni Frissell was well known for her innovative outdoor fashion photography. In fact, she was one of the first photographers to prefer outdoor photography to studio work. As a young woman, she too had spent summers in Newport and had learned to use a camera there in the 1930s. She liked to catch her subjects in a moment of pleasure or emotion, which is evident in the photographs of the Kennedy wedding she took for *Harper's Bazaar.*

Only a few brides are recorded for posterity by photographers of Toni Frissell's stature, but careful research and advance planning can result in wonderful photographs of your own celebration. Although it is a terrific idea to provide a single-use camera at each table for guests to take candid shots of the reception, avoid allow-

ing a well-meaning amateur photographer to take the official photographs. Instead, ask your wedding consultant, floral designer, or friends who have recently married to recommend a professional wedding photographer.

As Jackie understood so well, it is very important to work closely with a photographer so that he or she is able to capture the photos you want. The photographer should be given a list of the members of the wedding party and all relatives and out-of-town guests. A friend or attendant can be assigned to help the photographer locate these people at the reception. You won't regret paying for extra time and film to photograph the people who mean the most to you on this special day.

Paul "Red" Fay, an usher, shot a home movie of the Kennedy wedding with his 8-mm camera, the only record of its kind because this was in the days before professional videographers existed. As with photography, if you want a video of your wedding, hire a professional and discourage friends and relatives from bringing their own video cameras. Too many cameras whirring all over the place can make the celebration look like a television studio.

MEETING WITH THE PHOTOGRAPHER

❧ PRE-PLANNING. Before meeting with the photographer, find out if your church or synagogue has any restrictions involving photographing the ceremony itself. Prepare a list of "must-have" shots.

❧ PORTFOLIO. Most photographers are happy to show you their portfolios of past work. If you dislike a particular photographer's work, don't assume you can change his or her style by describing the particular look you want. What you see is what you'll get.

❧ FORMAL PORTRAITS. Many brides have the bridal portrait taken sometime before the wedding day. And others are setting aside the tradition of the groom not seeing the bride before the wedding and having their formal pictures taken at this time, too. Couples whose ceremony and reception are

Planning with the photographer before the wedding ensures that he or she will capture the moments, and the people, that matter most to you.

being held at the same location often have these photographs taken before their guests arrive. If your posed photos will take place at the reception, decide on a time with your photographer and make sure everyone in the wedding party knows where and when they should assemble for them.

❧ CANDID PHOTOS. Although Toni Frissell's photos of the Kennedy wedding were shot in the fifties, their casual, unposed simplicity looks very up-to-date. The trend today in wedding photography is to fewer posed shots and more candid pictures.

❧ COLOR OR BLACK AND WHITE. Black-and-white wedding photography has come back into vogue. Your photographer will need to know whether you want just color, just black and white, or a combination.

❧ NEGATIVES. Ask the photographer how long he or she keeps the negatives and if you can purchase them. If you buy the negatives, be prepared to pay a large sum of money for them, because wedding photographers make a profit on the sale of additional prints.

❧ ALBUMS. Usually three albums are ordered: one for the bride and groom, one for his parents, and one for her parents. The bride and groom take care of supplying prints to members of their wedding party. If they are very busy, one set of parents can take over the job. Usually the bride's family gives each member of the bridal party a color photograph of the group. Sometimes the bridesmaids' and ushers' gift from the bride and groom is a framed group photo of the wedding party. The attendants should pay for any additional photos they order.

❧ CONTRACT. The contract should specify the number and type of pictures to be taken, the time the photographer is to arrive, how long he or she will stay, the timetable for delivering the contact sheets to you, the timetable for delivering the finished prints that you order, the type of albums provided, and the cost.

Something Borrowed

At the Kennedy wedding reception, ice cream molds in the shape of roses
were served with the wedding cake. Perhaps the idea was inspired by Alice Roosevelt,
who served ice cream hearts at her 1906 wedding.

Jackie's gift to each of her bridesmaids was a monogrammed silver
picture frame; Jack's gift to each usher was a Brooks Brothers umbrella
with his initials and the wedding date engraved on the handle.

Tossing the bridal bouquet from a staircase landing
or balcony to the unmarried women guests below, as Jackie did,
provides a wonderful setting for photographs and gives
this sweet tradition a little more prominence.

Jackie loved to put together small books of her drawings,
reminiscences, and verse, foretelling her career as an editor later in
life. She made an inspirational one for her husband-to-be and
presented it to him on their wedding day. It bears an inscription
taken from Napoleon: "Great men are meteors,
consuming themselves to light the world."

Jackie's dark, wavy hair was worn off her face, with her lace headdress
and veil pinned to the back of her head. Hair worn down over the face can cast
shadows that might spoil an otherwise lovely wedding photo.

Jackie's flower girl, halfsister Janet Jennings Auchincloss,
wore a variation of the bridesmaids' dresses, with little-girl puff sleeves instead of
cap sleeves and a collar rather than a round neckline.

If you are considering black-and-white photography for your wedding,
vary the colors of your bridesmaids' dresses or include a deeper colored detail such as
a sash to add visual interest to the photographs.

CHAPTER SIX

FROM STAR TO PRINCESS

Having all of you here with me today makes all the difference in the world.

It reminds me that Rainier and I are just two people who love each other and are getting married.

Sometimes this week it's been hard to remember that. But looking at each one of my friends

at this moment makes everything very personal and very real.

— Grace Kelly

THE SIX BRIDESMAIDS hurried along the palace hallway to the gold and white salon where the official wedding photographs would be taken, their pale yellow organdy dresses floating gaily about them. Not far away, the bride was being helped into her elaborate gown, much as an Edwardian royal bride would have been half a century before.

Minutes later, when Grace Kelly entered the room, her attendants were struck by her incredible beauty. The exquisite wedding dress she wore accentuated her translucent skin, classic features, and cover-girl figure. It had been fashioned from twenty-five yards of silk taffeta, another twenty-five yards of silk *gros de longre* (a fabric that is no longer made), and three hundred yards of antique Valenciennes lace. Her lace-trimmed veil, which hung from a Juliet cap adorned with seed pearls, had been made from ninety yards of silk tulle. Not surprisingly, the bridal ensemble was heavy and awkward to wear, but Grace walked into the salon with the elegance and regal bearing of a born princess.

After photographs had been taken inside the palace, the bridesmaids joined Grace, her sister Peggy, who was matron of honor, and the six young attendants outside on a gallery overlooking the courtyard. For a moment, the bride stood alone at the balustrade and gazed out over the narrow, ancient streets of Monaco, her new home. Less than a year ago, in 1955, she had stood at the same spot on the first day she had met her husband-to-be, His Serene Highness Prince Rainier III.

Grace had been asked to head the American delegation to the Cannes Film Festival that May. She had recently won an Oscar for *The Country Girl* and was already famous for her roles in *Dial M for Murder*, *Mogambo*, and *Rear Window*. The Cannes job was mostly honorary, leaving her lots of time to visit with friends on the Riviera. Her meeting with the ruler of Monaco — a one-square-mile principality on the Mediterranean known mainly for its Monte Carlo casino — had been arranged in connection with the festival. But the day began disastrously.

When Grace woke up, she discovered that France's electrical workers had gone on strike the night before, leaving her with a closetful of wrinkled or unsuitable clothing. The only presentable dress was a black taffeta horror spotted with oversized pink and green roses. It hardly seemed appropriate for meeting royalty, but worse was yet to come. As she was about to leave her hotel, Grace was told that a hat was mandatory. All she could find were some artificial flowers, which were hurriedly twisted into her still-wet hair.

Two hours later, she and the *Paris Match* journalist who had helped set up the "photo opportunity" arrived at the prince's thirteenth-century castle, the Palais Princier — only to learn that Rainier was still entertaining friends at his villa down the coast.

(Opposite) In this famous photograph by *Life* magazine's Howell Conant, movie star Grace Kelly stands alone for a moment on the palace balcony before joining her bridesmaids for the short journey to the Cathedral of St. Nicholas — and to her new life as Princess Grace of Monaco.

When the thirty-one-year-old monarch finally arrived, he gave his American guest a tour of the palace gardens and his private zoo. During their short visit, he managed to charm Grace completely — and Grace, in return, impressed the dashing prince with her beauty, poise, and down-to-earth humor. "May must be my lucky month," Rainier later recalled. "I was born on the 23rd, came to the throne on the 9th and met Grace for the first time on the 6th." Without telling even their closest friends, they began to write each other long letters, which became more personal and revealing as the weeks went by.

By late summer of 1955, Grace's imaginary life in film began to mirror her personal life. In *The Swan*, she played Alexandra, a young commoner who is courted by a prince and must decide whether to accept his marriage proposal. That Christmas, Grace returned to Philadelphia to spend the holidays with her family — and with her prince. Rainier arrived on Christmas Day, and the young couple's feel-ings for each other quickly became apparent to all around them. When he proposed, the twenty-six-year-old star of her own fairy-tale romance did not hesitate to say yes.

Grace's friends were, of course, thrilled when they heard the news — but they were puzzled, too. Grace had always told them about her romantic involvements before, but she had said virtually nothing about Prince Rainier. Trying to explain her sudden engagement, Grace told her friend Judy Kanter, "He is everything I've ever loved. . . . I don't want to be married to someone who feels belittled by my success. . . . I couldn't bear walking into a restaurant and hearing the maître d' refer to my husband as Mr. Kelly." Later, she added, "I acted more on instinct, but then I always have. . . . We happened to meet each other at a time when each of us was ready for marriage. There comes a time in life when you have to choose."

On April 4, 1956, Grace, her family, three of her bridesmaids,

(Above) Grace and Prince Rainier stroll the grounds of the palace gardens. (Below left) Shortly after her engagement is made public,
the popular film star is mobbed by Hollywood reporters. (Below right) The bride-to-be arrives in Monaco for a week of festivities before the wedding.
(Opposite) The newly engaged couple at a party held in their honor at New York's Waldorf-Astoria.

and more than fifty friends set sail on the S.S. *Constitution* for Monaco and a week of festivities before the wedding. It was an exhilarating but exhausting week for everyone, filled with luncheons, formal dinner parties with exquisite food and vintage wines, a multitude of prying reporters everywhere they went, and even a jewel theft. In another case of life imitating art — this time, Grace's film *To Catch a Thief* — one of the bridesmaids had some expensive jewelry stolen from her hotel room. The hectic week ended on April 18 with the civil wedding ceremony required by law in Monaco, followed by a garden party for the entire adult population of the tiny principality — 3,000 guests and 3,000 slices of wedding cake! That night, the Monegasques celebrated the civil wedding of their ruler and his glamorous princess with a spectacular fireworks display.

The next morning, under a clear Mediterranean sky, the wedding party made its way from the palace through the crowded streets of Monaco to the magnificent Cathedral of St. Nicholas for the religious ceremony. Masses of white hydrangeas and fragrant lilies and lilacs filled the church and overflowed the altar. As the bridesmaids walked slowly up the aisle, followed by the flower girls and pages, the hundreds of famous guests — from Aristotle Onassis and Cary Grant to Ava Gardner and Gloria Swanson — turned to watch Grace enter the cathedral on her father's arm. She was breathtakingly beautiful and, throughout the long service, showed a tranquility and focus that her friends found amazing.

(Above) Grace Kelly's last public appearance, at the 28th Annual Academy Awards ceremony in March 1956. (Inset) An MGM poster advertising the official film of the royal wedding.

(Above) Grace leaves the palace on the arm of her father, John B. Kelly Sr., and is helped into a Rolls Royce by a liveried footman.

(Below) The bride arrives at the Cathedral of St. Nicholas. Prince Rainier arrived minutes later and, according to custom, followed his bride to the altar.

A sumptuous wedding luncheon for seven hundred guests followed the ceremony. The wedding party and family members sat at small tables for four in a reserved section of the palace courtyard while the rest of the guests served themselves from heavily laden buffet tables. Always a caring friend, Grace ensured that each of her bridesmaids spent a few moments with her and Rainier at their table during the reception. When it was time to cut the wedding cake — a six-tiered confection decorated with sugar replicas of the palace and topped with two cherubs and a crown — the honors were done with the prince's ceremonial sword.

After Grace had changed into her going-away outfit, she joined her bridesmaids in her sitting room. Her hairdresser, Virginia Darcy, came into the room behind Grace and laughingly said, "Come on, girls. Let's all curtsy to the new princess." It was an emotional moment, and they all found themselves fighting back tears. Each of them knew that Grace was embarking on a life that would, in many ways, take her out of their lives forever.

Later, from the battlements of the palace, the six bridesmaids watched quietly as Monaco's new royal couple sailed off in Rainier's white yacht, the *Deo Juvante*, followed by a flotilla of small boats. A few handfuls of rice were tossed into the air to wish them well. Judith Balaban Quine wrote of that moment, ". . . I felt something very strong and very deep. Something for each of us, separately, and for all of us together. Something that would bind me to these women for life. Perhaps it was merely our love for Gracie and her love for us. If so, that seemed enough."

(Opposite) A breathtakingly beautiful Princess Grace displays the poise that made her a Hollywood legend. (Above) Grace, Rainier, and the attendants during the solemn nuptial high mass celebrated by the Bishop of Monaco. (Below) The bridesmaids take turns enjoying a few moments with the royal couple.

*To see Grace was like seeing a statue
of alabaster marble. I have never seen anything
so exquisite in my life.*

— Earl Blackwell

(Opposite) A radiant Princess Grace and her husband wave to the crowds from the palace balcony.
(Above) The official wedding portrait. Although the world's top fashion designers
had vied for the honor of creating the royal wedding gown, Grace chose Hollywood designer
Helen Rose, who had recently designed the actress's gowns for the film *High Society*.

THE ATTENDANTS

We darted about the room, helping one another fasten buttons,

fluff petticoats and set hats at exactly the right angle.

— Judith Balaban Quine, The Bridesmaids

GRACE CHOSE her bridemaids from the friends she had made throughout her life — one was a close friend from high school days, two had attended the American Academy of Dramatic Arts with her, another had met her at the Barbizon Hotel for Women in New York, and two had been introduced to her by their husbands (one husband was Grace's agent and the other, her director on a television show). They were a lovely mix of old childhood friends, college chums and friends from work, with the addition of a sister as her matron of honor. Married bridal attendants were not common in Europe, yet five of Grace's were married and two were divorced. That she included them in her royal wedding is a measure of the loyalty she felt for her friends.

THE BRIDE'S ATTENDANTS

Hundreds of years ago, the first bridesmaids escorted the bride to the wedding, served as witnesses at the ceremony, and helped in the wedding preparations or at the wedding itself. Then, as now, probably one of the most difficult tasks facing a bride was choosing her attendants. Luckily, a few simple guidelines can eliminate, or at least reduce, hurt feelings.

The size of the wedding, for example, helps determine the number of attendants. For a small wedding, you might invite a sister or your best single friend to be your maid of honor — or a married sister or a close married friend to be your matron of honor. For a medium-sized wedding (up to 150 guests), six or fewer is the usual number of attendants. And for a large wedding (350 guests or more), you might consider having ten bridesmaids — including a maid or matron of honor — a junior bridesmaid, a ring bearer, and a flower girl. (More than ten bridesmaids, and they begin to look like a line of Rockettes from New York's Radio City Music Hall!)

If you come from a large family, invite either all your siblings or just one to be an attendant. Much older siblings will not expect to be included in the wedding party, but a younger sister (nine to thirteen years old) will undoubtedly enjoy being a junior bridesmaid. Asking a step- or a half-sibling to be an attendant is a wonderful way to further knit a remarried family together.

In choosing your other attendants, you might ask a sister of the groom or a few of your closest friends. If you have to leave out good friends, be sure to talk to them about it, emphasizing how much their friendship means to you. Ask them to help you with some aspect of the wedding and make sure they're invited to the pre-wedding parties, if possible. Having an attendant to whom you're not really close is often a mistake. This can put her in the embarrassing position of having to pretend she's a great friend of yours when she's not. Even having just one attendant is perfectly fine, especially if that person is very important to you and has stood by you throughout your life.

Sometimes a friend may accept your invitation to be a bridesmaid — with a significant "but" attached. She may not be able to afford the cost of the dress, any travel expenses there may be, or her share of the attendants' joint wedding gift. If her presence at your wedding really matters to you, make an effort to ease the financial costs for her. Perhaps you might ask one of your relatives to cover your friend's expenses, in lieu of a wedding gift.

THE GROOM'S ATTENDANTS

The groom usually has only one honor attendant, his best man, who is often his brother or best friend. However, Prince Rainier departed from tradition and had three witnesses — two close friends and Grace's brother, Kell. More recently, England's Prince Edward also set custom aside by asking both his brothers to be "supporters" at his 1999 wedding to Sophie Rhys-Jones.

The ushers, who are usually about the same age as the groom, are chosen from the groom's and bride's brothers and from the groom's close friends. In choosing his ushers, the groom should try to match the number of bridesmaids, but if he has fewer attendants than his bride, it really does not make any difference. At a very small wedding, it is nice to include a younger usher (aged ten or older), particularly if it is the bride's or groom's son by a previous marriage.

DUTIES OF THE BRIDE'S ATTENDANTS

MAID OF HONOR

❧ Organizes the joint gift for the bride, and may host or help plan a bridal shower

❧ Helps run errands for the bride before the wedding

❧ Looks after the bride's "revival" bag of makeup, hairbrush, safety pins, facial tissues, painkillers, breath mints, and other necessities

❧ Makes sure the bride's going-away outfit and luggage are delivered safely to the room where she will dress after the reception

❧ Helps the bride get dressed on the wedding day, and straightens her veil and train throughout the day

❧ Holds the groom's wedding band and the bridal bouquet during the ceremony

❧ May make a toast at the rehearsal dinner or wedding reception

❧ Ensures that the bridal gown is carefully returned to the bride's home after the couple has left the reception

BRIDESMAIDS

❧ Assist the bride and mother-of-the-bride with errands

❧ Guide the children in the wedding party during the processional and recessional

❧ Help collect gifts, floral arrangements, and possessions from the ceremony and reception sites

DUTIES OF THE GROOM'S ATTENDANTS

THE BEST MAN

❧ Organizes the ushers for fittings

❧ Informs the ushers of their duties and, on the wedding day, makes sure they are wearing their boutonnieres, have their seating lists in hand, and arrive an hour before the ceremony

❧ Organizes the joint groom's gift

❧ Helps arrange the bachelor party, at which the groom's and ushers' gifts are exchanged

❧ Ensures that the groom arrives for the ceremony, properly dressed, twenty minutes to half an hour beforehand

❧ Holds the bride's wedding band during the ceremony

❧ Ensures that the wedding license and payments for the officiant are taken to the ceremony

❧ Helps the mother-of-the-bride arrange transportation

❧ Makes the first toast to the bride at the rehearsal dinner and at the reception, and organizes the order of toasting that follows

❧ Oversees the transfer of the honeymoon luggage to the departure car, and ensures that the groom has travel plans and tickets

❧ Returns the groom's wedding suit (if rented) the day after the wedding

THE USHERS

❧ Escort guests to their seats at the religious ceremony

❧ Dance with the bride and all the bridesmaids

❧ Decorate the car in which the couple departs

OUTFITS FOR THE ATTENDANTS

THE BRIDAL ATTENDANTS

Although the pale yellow dresses worn by Princess Grace's attendants probably were not added to their wardrobes after the wedding, today's bridesmaids' gowns — with simple lines that echo day and evening dress styles — are more likely to enjoy a longer social life. But even if a bride chooses outfits that will only be worn once, she should pick affordable dresses, or skirts and tops, that her friends will feel good wearing on that one special day. Rather than shopping with her bridesmaids first — guaranteed to lead to disagreement and confusion — the bride should choose a few ensembles on her own and then return to the shop with her attendants to show them her choices.

Attendants no longer need to be dressed alike, but they should present a unified look that complements the bride. For example, if the bride wears a very simple gown, her attendants look best in simple dresses, too. A formal evening wedding in the fall or winter calls for dresses in heavier fabrics such as brocade and velvet, perhaps with matching jackets or wraps. At an informal spring or summer wedding, dresses in lovely lightweight fabrics such as chiffon, organza and silk crepe are more appropriate. Whatever the style, neither the bride's nor the bridesmaids' dresses should be overly revealing if the ceremony is to be held in a house of worship.

The figure types and personal styles of the attendants should also be taken into account. Straight skirts may not look good on everyone, while A-line skirts usually do. Sometimes a dress will be

(Opposite) Designed in a classic A-line silhouette with a choice of complementary fabrics and necklines, these dresses will provide a lovely and unified look for the wedding party — while flattering the individual characteristics of each bridesmaid.

Grace, too, had gifts for her attendants. Tearfully she told us

how much it meant to her to share her happiness with close friends during her wedding week.

Then she handed each of us a small jeweler's box containing a large gold charm.

— Judith Balaban Quine, *The Bridesmaids*

available with several different styles of neckline and shoulder treatments. Attendants can then choose the one they feel most comfortable wearing. If an attendant does not fit the standard sizes available in a particular dress style, the bride can take a sample dress to a dressmaker and have it specially made for a very tall or heavy bridesmaid.

Accessories can be coordinated after the dresses are chosen. Although shoes do not need to be the same style, if they are to be dyed, they should all be done at the same time and place to ensure that the same dye lot is used on all of them. The presence of a hair and make-up professional is almost a necessity for a large wedding to unify the look of the bride and her attendants. And finally, in trying to organize the accessories — hair decorations, flowers, hats, jewelry, handbags — don't forget little things like nail polish and hosiery.

THE GROOMSMEN

Fortunately, clothing choices for the groom and his groomsmen have returned to the classic styles of the past, which make every man look splendid. The groom's suit should vary slightly from his attendants' (the stripe down the leg of his trousers, for example, may be different) so that he stands apart from them, but the rest of the group should be identically dressed.

The formality of the wedding, the time of day or evening, the number of bridesmaids and, of course, the bride's dress all play a role in determining the apparel of the groom and his attendants. If, for example, the wedding is informal and the bride wears a short dress or suit, the men may wear black, dark blue or dark gray business suits with white shirts and gray or gray-striped ties. For a daytime summer wedding, dark blazers worn with white or gray trousers are always appropriate. For a formal white-tie evening wedding, full dress or tails is expected, including black tailcoat with white piqué waistcoat and bow tie, white shirt with wing collar, studs and cuff links. Top hats and white gloves may also be worn.

Shoes should be plain, undecorated and black, and worn with black dress socks. They should be unscuffed and polished. Black patent leather shoes are worn for a black-tie or white-tie evening wedding.

THANKING YOUR ATTENDANTS

Two evenings before the civil ceremony, Grace and Rainier invited the bridesmaids and their escorts to a private dinner at the palace. The six friends arrived an hour early to spend some time alone with Grace, and to give her their collective wedding present — an antique silver dressing-table set of mirror, brush, and comb engraved with her monogram and the inscription, "Remembrance of past happiness and wishes for future joy." After exchanging gifts, the women joined the men for an informal buffet dinner, albeit with

rare Meissen china, antique silver, and a dozen waiters, butlers, and footmen in livery! At the end of a memorable evening of delightful food, stories, word games and jokes, Judith Balaban Quine remembered parting "in the glow of everlasting friendship."

In the early 1900s, bridesmaids' luncheons were a wonderful opportunity for the bride-to-be to thank her friends for their help in planning her wedding. The dining room table would be covered with a long lace runner, a low china bowl of white carnations would be set in the center, and the bridesmaids' gifts would be wrapped in white paper tied with a white ribbon and decorated with a cut blossom. Lucky charms with ribbons attached would be placed between the layers of the cake served for dessert. Each bridesmaid would then gather around the cake before it was cut and pull a ribbon to tell her fortune: an engagement ring (next to marry), an anchor (travel), heart (love will come), horseshoe (lucky in life). After

lunch, they would jump over twelve lit candles, one for each month of the year. The one extinguished as each bridesmaid leaped over the flames would indicate in what month she would marry.

Whether you choose to hold a dinner party or an old-fashioned luncheon or tea for your attendants, this event celebrates friendship and is always a fun-filled way to thank your friends and relatives for their help in planning your wedding.

GIFTS FOR ATTENDANTS

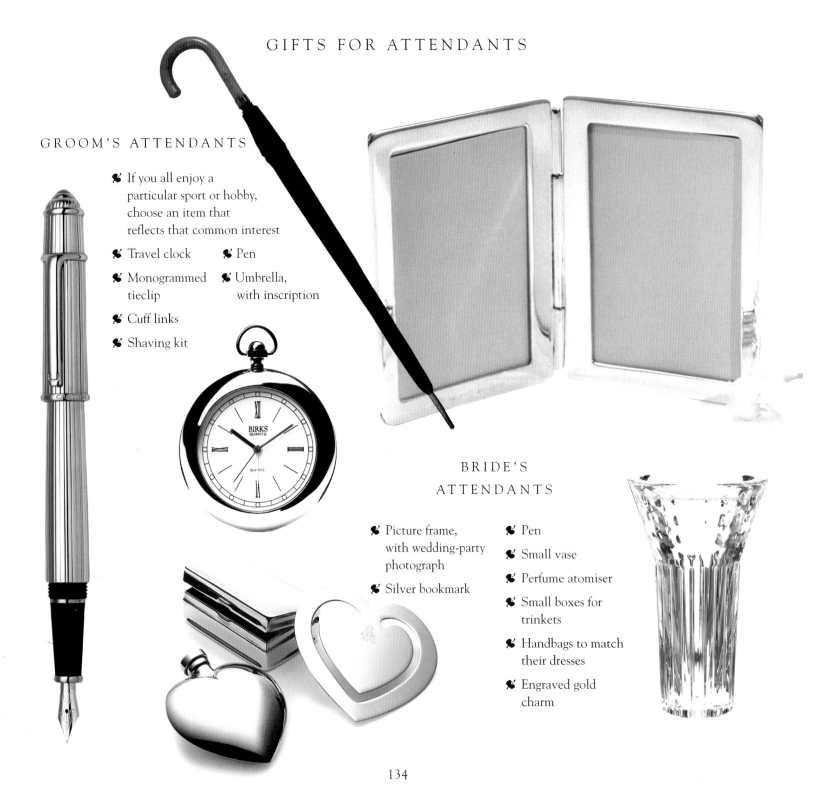

GROOM'S ATTENDANTS

- If you all enjoy a particular sport or hobby, choose an item that reflects that common interest
- Travel clock
- Pen
- Monogrammed tieclip
- Umbrella, with inscription
- Cuff links
- Shaving kit

BRIDE'S ATTENDANTS

- Picture frame, with wedding-party photograph
- Pen
- Small vase
- Silver bookmark
- Perfume atomiser
- Small boxes for trinkets
- Handbags to match their dresses
- Engraved gold charm

Something Borrowed

Two days before the ceremony, Rainier drove
his bride-to-be to an enchanting French village high in the
mountains above Monaco. Stealing a moment to be alone with your
fiancé during the days leading up to the wedding gives
both of you a chance to catch your breath.

When Grace's attendants arrived at the
Hotel de Paris in Monaco, they were delighted by the
beautiful floral arrangements they found in their rooms.
If some of your attendants are coming from out of town,
make them feel welcome with a bouquet of flowers, a box of their
favorite candy, or some other thoughtful gift.

Grace's missal was covered with white silk,
then a layer of lace in which a cross of seed pearls had been sewn.
She carried it with a small spray of lily of the valley.

In keeping with the tradition of
"something blue," Grace had tiny blue satin bows
sprinkled over the petticoats of her gown.

Instead of choosing a bridesmaid's bouquet of roses in full bloom,
you might consider using rosebuds, as Grace did.

Two ring bearers were part of the royal wedding party — one to carry the bride's
wedding band and the other to carry the groom's.

Having a piece of jewelry crafted for your attendants,
as Grace did for her bridesmaids, or having a storebought piece engraved makes
your gift extra-special.

HOLLYWOOD WEDDINGS

1949

I Love Lucy
(Below) Lucille Ball, star of one of America's best-loved television shows, seals her second marriage to co-star Desi Arnez with a kiss.

1934   *1945*

Ginger Rogers & Lew Ayres
(Above left) Holding a sheaf bouquet of calla lilies, a Hollywood legend debuts in her new role as radiant bride.

From Child Star to Bride
(Above right) A decidedly grownup Shirley Temple stands outside the church with her husband, army sergeant George Agar Jr., following their Beverly Hills wedding.

Edith Head creates the Hollywood Bride
Oscar-winning designer Edith Head dressed the stars for decades. This glamorous bridal gown (left), created by her for the 1939 musical *Paris Honeymoon*, features a molded waistline, sheer bodice, and billowing skirt trimmed with rows of white velvet ribbon.

1949

Screen Idol Weds
(Above) As ten thousand adoring fans braved the January cold outside Rome's Church of Santa Francesca Romana, dashing film idol Tyrone Power and MGM starlet Linda Christian exchanged vows during a solemn ceremony that rivaled the pageantry of a Hollywood wedding.

Love and marriage on the silver screen

(Left) Sweet but sexy in a classic satin gown, Sandra Dee epitomized every teen girl's dream bride in the sixties romantic comedy, *If a Man Answers*. (Far right) Nearly thirty years later, megastar Julia Roberts captured hearts as the bridal southern belle in *Steel Magnolias*. (Right) In the nineties, the charming comedy *Four Weddings and a Funeral* (bottom) broke box-office records and revived the popularity of the big, formal wedding. Meg Ryan (top) captured the look of the nineties bride in *Prelude to a Kiss* — glamorous but understated in a simple dress and unadorned veil.

Hollywood legends star in their own wedding spectaculars

Natalie Wood & Robert Wagner
(Far left) The bride wore a dramatic lace scarf and short-sleeved jacket over a short dress as two of Hollywood's hottest young actors tied the knot at a simple church ceremony outside Phoenix, Arizona.

Elizabeth Taylor Weds Hotel Heir
(Top left) The beautiful young actress and her first husband, Conrad Nicholson Hilton Jr., arrive at their lavish wedding reception at the Bel-Air Country Club in Beverly Hills.

Marilyn Monroe & Joe DiMaggio
(Bottom left) The storybook romance of the Blonde Bombshell and the Yankee Clipper culminated in the wedding of the decade. Although their marriage only lasted from January to October, the two remained friends.

Audrey Hepburn
With her striking beauty and unforgettable style, Audrey Hepburn was a breathtaking bride, both off-screen and on — (right) posing for the press in a wedding gown by Zoe Fontana of Rome, and with Fred Astaire in *Funny Face* (left).

1950

1951

1954

CHAPTER SEVEN

A RETURN TO ROMANCE

We want to make her look just like a fairy-tale princess.

— David Emanuel, co-designer of Diana's wedding dress

IN FEBRUARY 1979, Lady Diana Spencer was surprised to receive an invitation from the Prince of Wales to a house party at the royal estate of Sandringham. When she told Lucinda Craig Harvey, her friend exclaimed, "Gosh, perhaps you are going to be the next Queen of England!" To the eighteen-year-old Diana, the idea was unthinkable. "Can you see me swanning around in kid gloves and a ball gown?"

Diana had known Prince Charles all her life; in fact, it's not an exaggeration to say she was "the girl next door." Park House, her family's country residence, stood on the grounds of Sandringham. During the summer months, the young Royals liked to swim in the Spencers' pool, and Diana knew their mother well enough to call her Aunt Lilibet. The two families had always been close. Diana's father, Earl Spencer, served as an equerry to Queen Elizabeth, and her mother, Frances, had been a lady-in-waiting to the Queen Mother. But because Diana was thirteen years younger than the Prince of Wales, she was much better acquainted with Prince Andrew and Prince Edward than with their polo-playing older brother.

It wasn't until 1977, when Diana was sixteen, that Charles first noticed the "very amusing and jolly" youngest Spencer daughter. At that time the world's most eligible bachelor was dating Sarah, the eldest of the three Spencer girls. Although his relationship with Sarah ended the following year, he invited both Sarah and Diana to his thirtieth birthday party at Buckingham Palace. Then in 1979, when Diana was living in London and working part-time as a teaching assistant at the Young England kindergarten, she received the unexpected invitation to Sandringham.

Charles didn't show a serious interest in Diana, however, until the following year. At a July house party in the country, they sat next to each other at a barbecue, and after a while began to talk about the funeral of the Prince's favorite uncle, Lord Mountbatten. Diana told Charles, "You looked so sad when you walked up the aisle at the funeral. It was the most tragic thing I've ever seen. My heart bled for you when I watched it. I thought: 'It's wrong, you are lonely, you should be with somebody to look after you.'"

Diana's heartfelt comments obviously touched the Prince. More invitations quickly followed — to a performance at Royal Albert Hall, to a family weekend on board the royal yacht *Britannia* during the Cowes Week regatta, and to another family weekend at Balmoral, the royal family's retreat in Scotland. By the fall of 1980, Charles's courtship of "Shy Di" — as the media had dubbed the attractive blonde with the habitually downcast blue eyes — had begun in earnest.

In February 1981, Diana was preparing to leave on a trip to Australia to escape the relentless media attention surrounding her relationship with Charles. On February 6, shortly before her departure, the Prince invited her to Windsor Castle — and proposed!

(Opposite) Looking every inch a fairy-tale princess, Diana stands on the steps of St. Paul's Cathedral. Her gown of ivory silk taffeta and old creamy lace, with its delicate embroidery and frilled neckline and sleeves, captured the imagination of the world — and signaled the return of romantic bridal fashions.

Although Diana had already had a taste of the lack of privacy and tedium that royal life entails, she didn't hesitate to accept. She was a young woman in love, with the hopes and dreams of all brides-to-be.

When their engagement was officially announced on February 24, Diana became the first Englishwoman engaged to marry an heir to the throne in more than three hundred years. She also became the best-known bride-to-be of the century. From the moment rumors began to leak about the impending engagement, the smallest detail about Diana became news. The engagement ring Charles placed on her finger — a large sapphire encircled with diamonds and set in platinum — became the lead story on many television news programs. Whatever Diana wore or used, young women wanted. Jewelers were hard-pressed to keep enough sapphires in stock, and stores carrying makeup couldn't order her favorite color of eyeshadow fast enough to keep up with the demand.

Five months later, on July 28, 1981, Diana spent her last night as a commoner at Clarence House, the residence of the Queen Mother. From her window, she watched the enthusiastic crowds staking out their spots along the next morning's processional route, already gaily decorated with baskets of mauve, pink, and white petunias. During the evening, a signet ring decorated with the three-feather emblem of the Prince of Wales arrived with a note from Charles: "I'm so proud of you, and when you come up I'll be there at the altar for you tomorrow. Just look 'em in the eye and knock 'em dead."

Early the next morning, Diana confidently greeted her first visitors, hairdresser Kevin Shanley and his wife, Claire. Although the bride's signature layered hairstyle had already been copied around the globe, on her wedding day it would prove to be a bit too long and flyaway under the Spencer family tiara. Diana refused to have any hairspray touch it, and to the dismay of Mr. Shanley, absentmindedly took out her rollers as she talked on the phone to Charles, before her hair had dried completely.

While Diana's natural-looking makeup was applied, Nina Missetzis, the seamstress who had made the wedding dress for the House of Emanuel, waited patiently to fit the gown on Diana for the last time. The sumptuous silk taffeta dress, with its lace-trimmed puffed sleeves and frilled neckline, was encrusted with tiny pearls and sequins and had a twenty-five-foot-long train — the longest in royal wedding history. The train was matched by an equally long ivory tulle veil. For luck, a tiny diamond-studded gold horseshoe and a "something blue" bow had been sewn into the waistband. Although many fashion critics later commented that the dress was much too fussy, designers Elizabeth and David Emanuel had, in fact, perfectly captured the fairy-tale magic of the occasion. They had concocted a wedding gown fit for a storybook princess — the fabric was beautiful, the workmanship was exquisite, and the bride was breathtaking.

Mrs. Missetzis later recalled how Diana had gazed at herself in a mirror as she stood transformed from a kindergarten teacher into a fairy-tale princess. With tears in her eyes, she kissed the seamstress, "Oh thank you, Nina, thank you!" Her younger brother, Charles, who had popped in to provide moral support, remembered the moment in typical brotherly fashion: "It was the first time in my life I ever thought of Diana as beautiful. She really did look stunning that day and very composed. . . . "

Her Glass Coach awaited — the same one in which Queen Elizabeth rode years ago on her wedding day. Earl Spencer helped his daughter arrange the yards of tulle around her, and as they made their way slowly through the packed streets to St. Paul's Cathedral where twenty-five hundred guests waited, Diana sang to amuse her father and to keep herself calm. She was worried about the Earl, who was still recovering from a near-fatal stroke. Even the Queen had cautioned Diana's father about accompanying his daughter up the aisle: "Please do take your time, Johnny." After Diana and her father entered the famous domed cathedral and the first stirring notes of Jeremiah Clarke's "Trumpet Voluntary" began to play, Earl Spencer whispered, "Walk now, shall we? Here we go, go slowly."

(Opposite) During the two-mile procession to St. Paul's, a very relaxed Diana waves to the crowds from inside the gold-trimmed Glass Coach. (Above) As a gust of wind catches her elaborately embroidered tulle veil, Diana turns to smile one last time before climbing the steps of the cathedral on the arm of her father, Earl Spencer.

(Left) Prince Charles chose St. Paul's Cathedral — rather than Westminster Abbey, where royal and society weddings were usually held — because of its magnificent setting and spectacular acoustics. More than two thousand guests, including the crown heads of Europe and world statesmen, watched as Charles and Diana exchanged vows (above) in front of the Archbishop of Canterbury. (Below) Diana, with Charles beside her in full naval dress uniform, turns to acknowledge a well-wisher's comment as the couple leaves the cathedral.

As she walked up the aisle, Diana's eyes swept the beautifully dressed crowd. On the groom's side, in the third row from the front, she spotted Camilla Parker-Bowles. Years later, Diana told biographer Andrew Morton that as she had passed Charles's mistress, she had thought, "Well, let's hope that's all over with." At last they reached the altar and the Earl happily delivered his youngest daughter to her waiting groom.

Like so many nervous couples, Diana and Charles fluffed their vows — the bride mixing up her groom's names, and the groom agreeing to share his bride's worldly goods with her, but not his own. The wedding band Charles slipped on Diana's finger was fashioned from the same nugget of Welsh gold that had been used for the Queen Mother's, the Queen's, Princess Margaret's, and Princess Anne's wedding rings. The couple and their guests listened solemnly to the Archbishop of Canterbury's address, as he quoted the poet Edwin Muir: "Each asks from each other what each most wants to give and each awakes in each what else would never be." Afterward, the New Zealand opera singer Kiri Te Kanawa sang an aria from Handel's *Samson*, "Let the Bright Seraphim," and the St. Paul's Cathedral Choir sang the Parry anthem, "I Was Glad."

Finally, to Diana's relief — "Well, I'm glad that bit's over!" — it was time to walk down the aisle with her new husband to Elgar's "Pomp and Circumstance March no. 4" and Walton's "Crown Imperial."

Back at Buckingham Palace, the Prince and Princess of Wales waved to the ecstatic crowds below and kissed briefly, the first public kiss on the royal balcony. Former butler Paul Burrell recalled: "After that royal kiss she went against royal protocol, gathered her train in her arms, shed her satin slippers and ran barefoot down the length of the principal corridor. The wedding was not like the state occasion it appeared on the outside — it was friendly, warm, and giggly. Diana would tease the young bridesmaids and make jokes, encouraging them to be naughty."

Diana's country affectionately embraced its "English rose," as did the 750 million people around the world who watched on television as she married her prince. In hindsight, their marriage was not the stuff fairy tales are made of, but certainly the wedding of Charles, Prince of Wales, and Lady Diana Spencer represented a return to the romantic storybook ceremonies of the past. After more than a decade of informal, come-as-you-are weddings, people warmly welcomed a return to formality and tradition.

(Opposite) Surrounded by the Household Cavalry, the newlyweds travel in the open state landau from St. Paul's down Fleet Street and along the Strand.
(Above) Diana, now Princess of Wales, stands with Prince Charles on the balcony at Buckingham Palace as the jubilant crowds below roar their approval.

FLOWER GIRLS AND RING BEARERS

Little Clementine Hambro was heartily bored when the "soppy kissing" began.

The Churchillian spirit deserting her completely,

she rested her head on her arm but clung with the other hand to the bride.

— Ann Morrow, *Princess*

THAT DIANA had a genuine affinity for children was evident even in her early days as a teaching assistant. The European tradition of having children as the bride's attendants suited her, although it is said she would have liked to have had a few of her friends with her on her long journey up the aisle. Her future sister-in-law, Princess Anne, had opted for only two attendants at her 1973 wedding: her nine-year-old cousin, Lady Sarah Armstrong-Jones, and her nine-year-old brother, Prince Edward. Eight years later, the well-practiced Lady Sarah kept an eye on the four younger bridesmaids and two pages at Diana's wedding.

Including children in the wedding ceremony dates back to ancient times. At early Greek and Roman weddings, little girls sprinkled herbs and grains — symbols of fertility — in the bride's path. In the Middle Ages, the bride was preceded up the aisle by a pair of young girls carrying wheat sheaves. The sheaves were replaced by nosegays in Elizabethan times and by pretty baskets of rose petals or floral-decorated hoops in Victoria's day.

Including pages in the wedding party can be traced back to medieval times. Formally dressed, these young boys carry a bride's long train and are associated with very grand society or royal weddings.

Young attendants can be the bride's or groom's nieces or nephews, godchildren, or children of close friends. The ideal age for a flower girl or ring bearer is between five and eight years old, although children as young as three are often seen in wedding parties. Older girls — between the ages of nine and thirteen — are considered junior bridesmaids.

It is always a good idea to assign one of the bridesmaids to look after the youngest members of the wedding party. I will never forget one junior bridesmaid who suddenly left the processional to catch the ring bearer, her three-year-old brother, after he had run off into a pew. She scolded him and he obediently followed her back across the church and into the procession. The bridal party had come to a halt during this little drama. Everyone, including the bride, was laughing, but it did not detract in the slightest from the beauty of the wedding. It added to it.

My own grandson, Luke, was the ring bearer at a wedding in Virginia Beach. He handled things well until he neared the altar,

(Overleaf) Inside a palace hallway, the Queen looks on with motherly concern as Diana bends down for a reassuring word with her youngest attendant, four-year-old Clementine Hambro, great-granddaughter of Sir Winston Churchill. In keeping with the romantic style of Diana's gown, the bridesmaids wore ballerina-length Victorian-style dresses — with charming headwreaths of pink roses and yellow freesia entwined with ivy.

Dresses for flower girls
should always be in keeping with the
style of the wedding. Choose pretty
fabrics — such as silk satin,
soft organza, and tulle (or velvet
and lace for autumn and winter
weddings) — that complement the
bridal gown. And include subtle
details that little girls love —
fabric rosettes, organza ribbons,
pleats, or tiny covered buttons.

then he tossed the ring pillow aside (fortunately, it was caught and handed to the best man), crawled onto the first pew, and promptly fell asleep, even emitting an audible snore during the service. The guests were in stitches.

When children are part of the wedding party, the bride and groom must be prepared for unexpected behavior plus two other facts of life: children always have to go to the bathroom at just the wrong moment, and they inevitably steal the show. Couples who invite children to be flower girls or ring bearers need to be self-confident and to possess a good sense of humor.

Children, particularly girls, usually love being part of a wedding party, but it can still be a daunting experience. Like the other attendants, they should be given the chance to practice walking up the aisle at the rehearsal. On the wedding day, having a relative nearby as they wait their turn to join the processional provides someone they know to take care of them if they decide not to proceed. Letting them sit with their parents in one of the first pews after their "performance" is helpful as well. To keep their jobs as simple as possible, flower girls should be given their bouquet, basket, or old-fashioned floral hoop just before the processional begins. The ceremonial pillow, with the rings attached to it by tiny ribbons, should be given to the ring bearer at the same time.

OUTFITS FOR YOUNG ATTENDANTS

In keeping with the romantic style of Diana's lace-trimmed gown, her attendants wore ballerina-length dresses with gold silk taffeta sashes and lace flounces on the skirt and sleeves. Gold slippers matched their sashes. The white gloves and gold-trimmed, dark blue jackets of the two pages were copies of the 1863 full dress Royal Naval Cadets' uniforms and echoed the groom's naval attire.

Picking the outfits that will be worn by the children in the wedding party is one of the most pleasant tasks associated with planning a wedding. To present a unified look, the flower girls' outfits generally match the bridesmaids' in style; in other words, a classic sheath worn by the bride or her attendants calls for a simpler child's dress than a Victorian-inspired bridal gown would. Little boys are often dressed in age-appropriate suits in colors that match

GIFTS FOR YOUNG ATTENDANTS

Pretty barrettes, earrings, necklaces, or bracelets for flower girls

A model of the wedding car or limousine for ring bearers or pages

A keepsake album for photos, the invitation, and pressed flowers from the wedding

A signed and dated framed photo of the entire wedding party

what the groom and his attendants will be wearing. Scottish kilts are, of course, popular in Britain and have been worn there by little boys in wedding parties since Victoria's time. In choosing the outfits for both girls and boys, try to ensure that the clothing will be comfortable to wear — no tight collars or scratchy materials.

At the 1993 wedding of Prince Alois of Liechtenstein and Duchess Sophie of Bavaria, the flower girls and pages were dressed in summery white outfits trimmed with deep yellow. The long yellow sashes — tied behind in large bows — on the little girls' puff-sleeved dresses were repeated in the wide yellow belts of the little boys' short pants, worn with short-sleeved shirts. Beautiful white floral wreaths adorned the girls' heads.

Child attendants have worn floral headwreaths, a symbol of innocence, for more than two thousand years. Diana's floral designer made full wreaths of pink roses, yellow freesia, and ivy for the Princess's young attendants. Sarah Ferguson's flower girls wore half wreaths of sweetheart roses and lily of the valley. Other options include a single bloom, a hair ribbon, or a decorated headband. A ring bearer's boutonniere can be a small blossom of one of the flowers in the flower girls' bouquets, or a smaller version of the groomsmen's boutonnieres. His ring pillow often matches the fabric of the flower girls' dresses.

Something Borrowed

Diana chose an ivory silk paper taffeta for her dress to complement the
creamy heirloom lace that would be used. The color also flattered her complexion,
which tended to redden with any excitement.

Just in case it rained on the royal wedding day, an antique parasol,
covered in silk and lace to match Diana's dress, was prepared.

The soles of Diana's ivory silk wedding shoes
were made of suede so that she wouldn't slip — another
sensible precaution. Young attendants' shoes
should also have non-skid soles.

Including a beloved relative's favorite
flower in your bouquet, as Diana did in honor of
Prince Charles's uncle, Lord Mountbatten,
is a sweet and touching gesture.

Royal photographer Patrick Lichfield took
several close-up photographs of the Princess of Wales
alone, which made her face — rather than
her elaborate gown — the focal point of the picture.
You might consider a close-up shot when
while you are looking your very best.

The night before Diana and Charles's wedding,
a fireworks display set to Handel's *Music for the Royal Fireworks* was held in London's Hyde Park.
Fireworks can lend a festive air to an outdoor wedding reception, too.

You can be sure that members of royal families signed the wedding
register with a beautiful pen. You might consider buying a vintage fountain pen to use
for special occasions throughout your married life.

CHAPTER EIGHT

AN IDYLLIC PLACE
FOR A WEDDING

It was important for us to be able to conduct this in a private,

prayerful and meaningful way with the people we love.

— John F. Kennedy Jr.

THE WEDDING of Carolyn Bessette to America's most eligible bachelor was not at all what Hollywood and the celebrity press would have planned for the couple. Privacy, simplicity, and understatement marked the arrangements. It all added up to quiet good taste — a quality unknown to many of the people who plan celebrity weddings today.

After Senator Edward Kennedy revealed to the press that his nephew John had secretly wed Carolyn on September 21, 1996, I told a journalist, "Jackie must be smiling in heaven." I'm sure she would have enjoyed her son's small, private wedding on a remote barrier island off the coast of Georgia. It was the type of wedding she would have liked for herself. The celebration's romantic seaside setting — not to mention the cloak-and-dagger planning preceding it — would undoubtedly have appealed to her.

The toddler I knew during my years in the Kennedy White House grew up to be a handsome, accomplished man, known for his polished manners and his warm, immediate-response thank-you notes. He was a genial person, without airs, but with an undeniably aristocratic bearing. John once said in an interview that his mother had taught him "decency, honesty, and compassion." And from all accounts, she taught him well. After graduating from Brown University, John attended New York University Law School, graduating in 1989. He briefly worked as an assistant district attorney before

leaving the law to launch the political magazine *George* in 1995.

Like his mother, John craved exercise. He walked, biked, rollerbladed, swam, or ran every day of his life. In New York's Central Park, he attracted the admiring glances of every woman he jogged past. In 1993, a friend introduced him to a lovely blonde on one of the footpaths. Carolyn Bessette was tall, slim, and, like Jackie, stylish, beautiful, and sophisticated. At the time, she worked as a publicist for designer Calvin Klein. As part of her job, Carolyn served as a personal shopper for celebrities and socialites. A few weeks after literally running into her, John visited Carolyn at work, staying long enough to buy three suits. Soon *People* magazine's "sexiest man alive" and the tall glamorous blonde became inseparable.

In 1995, John and Carolyn began living together in a loft in Manhattan's trendy TriBeCa district, where they were often seen walking their dog or rollerblading. Evenings of parties, theater, or charity events, weekends at the Martha's Vineyard house that John had inherited from Jackie, and short holidays in Paris and Honduras rounded out the couple's pleasant days spent together. That August, John gave Carolyn an emerald-and-diamond engagement ring reminiscent of the one his father had given his mother. Publicly they denied they were engaged, but privately they began to plan their quiet wedding away from the spotlight.

The couple turned to some of their closest friends for help.

As night falls on Cumberland Island, John Kennedy Jr. and Carolyn Bessette exchange their wedding vows by the soft glow of an oil lamp.
A single candle on the altar of the rustic church offers the only other illumination.

(Above) The stately turn-of-the-century Greyfield Inn, with its avenue of moss-covered trees, recalls an earlier time of gentility and grace. (Below) The island's windswept dunes appealed to John's love of the sea, and offered the young couple privacy, freedom, and peace. (Opposite) The verandah of the inn, where the rehearsal dinner took place.

Gordon Henderson, a clothing designer and former colleague of Carolyn's, designed John's wedding attire — a midnight blue wool suit worn with a white piqué vest. He also helped Carolyn choose the beautiful tablecloths for the rehearsal dinner. Janet "Gogo" Ferguson, a jewelry designer, helped with the logistics of holding the wedding at a remote destination and also created the couple's unique wedding rings. Professional photographer Denis Reggie, Ted Kennedy's brother-in-law, took the photographs. Fashion designer Narciso Rodriguez created Carolyn's exquisite wedding dress and the beaded chiffon frock she wore for the rehearsal dinner. Family friend and Jackie's longtime butler, Efigenio Pinhiero, lent a hand by decorating the island's tiny church with wildflowers and grapevines. Everyone, of course, was sworn to secrecy.

Cumberland Island's remoteness, tranquillity, and natural beauty make it an ideal choice for a secret hideaway. Populated by wild horses, countless birds, and fewer than fifty people, the eighteen-mile-long island has been preserved as a National Seashore and is accessible only by boat or plane. Its sole communications link to the mainland is by cell phone, and the only vehicles allowed onshore are owned by either the Park Service or the permanent residents.

The one hotel on Cumberland, the exclusive Greyfield Inn, was opened by Janet Ferguson's family in 1962. The Fergusons are descendants of steel magnate Thomas Carnegie, who once owned the entire island. The inn's turn-of-the-century clapboard mansion, built for Carnegie's daughter Margaret, stands on two hundred very private wooded acres overlooking a pristine white-sand beach. John had become friends with the Fergusons on visits to Cumberland Island beginning in the 1980s. "We had the pleasure of getting to know Carolyn a couple of years before they got married," Janet Ferguson told *The Atlanta Journal and Constitution*. "She started coming down to the island, too. It was a place where both of them could have privacy together." Not surprisingly, they chose this idyllic spot, with its grand inn and fond memories, for their wedding.

John and Carolyn invited about forty guests to the ceremony and reception. Many of the Kennedy cousins were not invited, which hurt their feelings because John went to all of the Kennedy "doings." He was a good sport, but he was not a politician, and he and his bride obviously felt that this wedding was theirs, not the clan's.

About twenty of their closest friends and family members arrived the night before the wedding and were put up at either the inn or one of the family homes graciously offered to the Kennedys by the Fergusons. The twenty or so remaining guests arrived the next day by plane or ferry. That afternoon, inn employees drove the guests along the beach at low tide — a faster, more comfortable route than the rutted one-lane road — to First African Baptist Church at the north end of the island. While the bride and groom changed into their wedding clothes at a nearby house, their guests explored the area around the wooden church — the adults admiring the wild horses cared for by a local naturalist, and the children looking for armadillos under the pines.

As the sun began to set, a single candle was lit in front of the small driftwood cross on the church's rustic altar. A neighbor's oil lamp and a flashlight on loan from the Park Service provided the only other illumination in the small room, now crowded with expectant guests. When the signal was given for the processional to begin, John's nieces — eight-year-old Rose and six-year-old Tatiana — wearing tea-length, white linen dresses, scattered rose petals as they proceeded slowly up the aisle. The proud ring bearer, their three-year-old brother, John, reached the front pew and, to everyone's amusement, exclaimed, "Why's Carolyn all dressed up like that?"

The bride stood at the back of the church, her pearl-colored silk crepe dress shimmering in the soft light. A panel at the back

floated behind her in a suggestion of a train. "Carolyn is a rare beauty, and I wanted the dress to be a frame for that beauty," designer Narciso Rodriguez told *InStyle* magazine. Crystal-beaded silk satin sandals, long white silk gloves, and a simple veil of hand-rolled silk tulle completed the willowy twenty-nine-year-old's sleek wedding look — an unadorned style that continues to appeal to young brides and to influence wedding gown design today.

At the altar, Carolyn held hands with John. Beside them stood her matron of honor, Caroline Kennedy Schlossberg, in a navy blue silk crepe gown (also designed by Rodriguez), and the best man, John's cousin, Anthony Radziwill. Family friend Rev. Charles O'Byrne conducted the Catholic service, during which passages of Scripture were read by members of both families. The only music was provided by David Davis, an elementary schoolteacher and gospel singer from a nearby town on the mainland. He sang, *a capella*, two hymns chosen by John and Carolyn — "Amazing Grace" during the processional and "Will the Circle Be Unbroken" during the recessional. His magnificent voice filled the little church, causing the guests to break into spontaneous applause at the end of the last hymn — as much for his singing as for the happy couple walking down the aisle.

Outside, the newlyweds stood against a fence while Denis Reggie took more photographs. To the delight of everyone watching, one of Cumberland's wild horses strolled up and nibbled Carolyn's bouquet of lily of the valley. Everyone then climbed back into the inn's vehicles and returned along the beach to Greyfield for the reception.

Circular tents with oak dance floors had been erected under the trees. The guests dined on shrimp, grilled swordfish, and artichokes, followed by lemon-raspberry ice cream and a three-tiered, vanilla-buttercream-frosted wedding cake decorated with fresh flowers. Ted Kennedy proposed the first toast to the new Kennedy couple, bringing tears to many eyes. In a statement to the press issued a few days after the wedding, he said, "I know Jack and Jackie would be very proud of them and full of love for them as they begin their future together."

The world saw the photographs of the couple and gasped at the sheer poetry of the two figures standing in the glow of candlelight at the doorway of the little church. Suddenly, glitzy plastic weddings seemed very tired and pedestrian. Couples and their parents began checking out every private island they could find to switch the locale of their weddings from the mundane local church and banquet facilities. Brides-to-be all over the world discarded their beaded, bouffant wedding dresses for the slinky slip dress worn by Carolyn. The only trouble was that Carolyn's dress could only be worn by someone as slim as she was.

Sadly, only three years later, Senator Kennedy would give another family statement to the press after the death of John and Carolyn in a plane crash. He remembered them as having "their own special brand of magic that touched everyone who knew and loved them." Ironically, the crowds of onlookers and press they had escaped so artfully on Cumberland Island surrounded them in death. But even though throngs of people filled the roads around Hyannis Port, the couple was buried at sea with just their families present.

When news of the marriage of America's most eligible bachelor to Carolyn Bessette was made public, this iconic photograph by Denis Reggie — one of only two wedding images released to the media — was immediately published in newspapers and magazines around the world. It is reproduced here exactly as the photographer shot it.

DESTINATION WEDDINGS

I knew that [getting married on Cumberland] was going to be logistically very hard to do. . . . But I also knew that it was the one gift that I could give two friends that no one could give to them. It was their privacy.

— Janet Ferguson, quoted in *The Atlanta Journal and Constitution*, 1999

IN PREPARATION FOR their romantic wedding on Cumberland Island, John and Carolyn had to arrange for a special-use permit from the National Park Service, a Georgia marriage license, blood tests, ferry reservations, an officiant, and a place to stay. Fortunately, they had a friend on-site who looked after many of the details for them. Although it was complicated to arrange, a destination wedding fulfilled their desire to have a private, intimate celebration away from the media spotlight.

Other couples like the idea of enjoying a wonderful holiday setting for a few days with their closest family members and friends. In fact, even weddings held close to home have been expanding from one-day events into weekend celebrations — with a Friday rehearsal dinner, a Saturday wedding ceremony, and a Sunday brunch. Spending the wedding weekend on a tropical island simply adds to the magic and excitement of the occasion. According to *Modern Bride*, the most popular off-shore destinations for American couples are Hawaii, the U.S. Virgin Islands, Jamaica, Bermuda, St. Lucia, and the Bahamas.

Flying to Europe or farther afield for the wedding weekend has become something of a trend among wealthy young Americans looking for unusual or exotic places to hold their weddings. At most of these events, a few hundred guests zip across the Atlantic to celebrate with the happy couple — a trend begun by the daughters of American billionaire Robert Miller in the early nineties. The wedding of Miller's daughter Pia to Christopher Getty took place in Bali, followed three years later by that of her sister Chantal to Crown Prince Pavlos of Greece in England.

For those of more modest means, choosing a destination,

DECORATING WITH CANDLES

Candles bring a romantic softness and intimacy to the lighting at the wedding ceremony and the reception.

❧ Candlelit ceremonies in the late afternoon or evening are once again in vogue with many of today's brides. Candle stands on either side of the altar and at the ends of pews traditionally decorate many places of worship for weddings, but check with your officiant to find out what the building's fire regulations are.

❧ The same applies for the reception site. Floating candles or votives in clear bowls or candles in glass containers are safer than open flames.

They are also less likely to be extinguished when used outdoors or in rooms with opened windows.

❧ Unscented candles are preferable. Aromatic ones can overpower the wonderful fragrance of your flowers and can alter the taste of the food being served at the reception.

deciding on the number of guests, if any, and setting a budget are the major steps in planning an out-of-town wedding. John and Carolyn flew to Turkey for their honeymoon, but many couples choose the same location for their wedding ceremony and honeymoon. (This is becoming so popular that Sandals Resorts has coined the term "weddingmoon" to describe it.)

Enlisting the help of a travel agent and wedding planner makes the planning much easier. Some large travel agencies have special departments designed to help with organizing a wedding abroad, and about a dozen cruise lines also offer on-board or shore-side wedding ceremonies. Resorts and hotels that specialize in destination weddings often have a wedding planner on-site, or ask your travel agent to recommend a local one in the place you've chosen.

The destination wedding planner should be able to arrange for the marriage license and any other necessary legal papers, accommodation, the setting for the ceremony, the officiant, the reception, the cake, photographer, flowers, and hair stylist. A contract setting out the arrangements and rates you have agreed on is a necessity. All-inclusive wedding and honeymoon packages from resorts, cruise lines, or tour operators should be checked carefully for add-on costs such as taxes and activity fees. Ask about credit card discounts, off-season rates, and videos to give you a sense of past weddings arranged by a resort or wedding planner.

Most couples invite a small number of guests, or none at all, to their destination wedding. For this reason, safeguarding against hurt feelings becomes a key consideration. Common sense dictates, for example, that you cannot invite one set of parents and not the other. To placate disappointed family and friends, many couples hold a party in celebration of their wedding after their return.

Although a wonderful gesture, paying for their guests' travel and accommodation expenses is not an option for most couples. This may mean that some people you invite will not be able to attend. Others may plan a holiday around your wedding. If this is the case, you can provide brochures and information to help your guests plan their time once the wedding festivities are over. When your guest list is confirmed, reserve everyone's rooms and ensure that their visas, passports, and inoculations are in order.

Destination weddings — whether held in a Scottish castle, a Mexican *casita*, or on a private beach in the Caribbean — are appealing to more and more couples each year. And John and Carolyn's Cumberland Island wedding set the standard for these romantic weddings far from home.

Something Borrowed

The large porch of a heritage home or inn is a wonderful setting
for a small rehearsal or wedding dinner. John and Carolyn held their dinner on Greyfield's
wide porch under an enormous oak tree. Candles provided the only illumination,
helped by the sparkle of crystal, silverware, and china plates.

When planning a destination wedding with guests, it's a nice idea to arrange an
activity to follow the rehearsal dinner. John and Carolyn's guests were invited to join the
couple for dessert, cognac, and cigars at the inn's beach gazebo, which was lit by tiki torches stuck
in the sand. Afterward, everyone gathered around a large bonfire by the water's edge.

John and Carolyn chose "Forever in My Life" by Prince
for their first dance — a non-traditional choice but obviously a song they had
enjoyed listening and dancing to in the past.

Simple one-flower bouquets, like Carolyn's lily-of-the-valley posy, look striking
against an unembellished gown.

Brides don't have to be the only ones wearing "something borrowed."
John wore his father's watch and a pair of JFK's cufflinks to his wedding ceremony.

ACKNOWLEDGMENTS

I AM IMMENSELY grateful to Hugh Brewster, Laurie Coulter, and Wanda Nowakowska of Madison Press Books for producing a beautiful book and an important piece of social history flavored with romance — at a time when it has never been more needed. Susan Barrable and Donna Chong are the two heroines of the production of this book, and I thank them, too, as well as Gord Sibley and Dale Vokey, who designed this book so that it's a note of grace at every bedside and on every coffee table.

My thanks, too, to Romona Keveza, the talented designer who generously provided her bridal gowns and has contributed so much to this project. And to Peter Duchin, one of America's best-loved dance music magicians and wedding music authorities, my thanks for all the conversations in which we spun a few memories, and had a few laughs which we can't share because we'd be sued! My thanks go also to everyone who supplied the historical and contemporary photography that make these pages glitter. Without these images to help us remember, there would be no understanding of what it was like. And what it was like was very special — as you'll see when you go through these pages.

— *Letitia Baldrige*

MADISON PRESS BOOKS would like to single out Cile Bellefleur-Burbidge and John Burbidge, Romona Keveza, Karina Lemke of Posies Flower Shop, Kim Ironmonger of Valencienne, and Janis Nicolay of Wedlock Photography for their wise advice, enthusiasm and generosity throughout the course of this project. We truly could not have done this book without them. Special thanks also go to Davina Abdallah of Birks, Glenn Bradie of the Everett Collection, Jason Barnett of *Coastal Living*, Darragh Caplan of *WeddingBells*, Stephanie Carron of Lavender Press, Susan Chin of Liaison Agency, Patrick Cuccaro of Affairs to Remember Caterers, Sue Daly and Matthew Weigman of Sotheby's, Deborah Fiddy of Harrods, Martine Frost of The Constance Spry Flower School, Allan Goodrich of the Kennedy Library, Diane Kirkland of Georgia Tourism, Julia Kleyner of Tiffany & Co., Laurie Kratochvil of *InStyle*, Jenny Luker of Platinum Guild International, Phyllis Magidson of the Museum of the City of New York, Andy Marcus of Fred Marcus Photography, Jenna Muirhead-Gould, Bruce Russell, Arlete Santos of Archive Photos, Suzanne Shutts of the Pink Beach Club, Priscilla Wannamaker, and Zachary Zoul of Greyfield Inn.

LIST OF SOURCES

CAKES

Cile Bellefleur-Burbidge
12 Stafford Road
Danvers, MA 01923-2539
Tel: (978) 774-3158

Bonnie Gordon Cakes
8 Gilgorm Road
Toronto, Ontario M5N 2M5
Tel: (416) 484-8499
www.bonniegordoncakes.com

Cliff Simon Cakes
1300 S Pleasant Valley Road
Suite 161
Austin, TX 78741
Tel: (512) 428-9366
www.webart.com/cake

Gail Watson Custom Cakes
335 West 38th Street
New York, NY 10018
Tel: (212) 967-9167
www.gailwatsoncake.com

Sylvia Weinstock Cakes
273 Church Street
New York, NY 10013
Tel: (212) 925-6698

CATERERS AND EVENT PLANNERS

Affairs to Remember
680 Ponce De Leon Avenue
Atlanta, GA 30308
Tel: (404) 872-7859
www.affairs.com

Event Design Group
4490 Commerce Drive
Atlanta, GA 30336
Tel: (404) 696-4737
www.eventdesigngroup.com

DESTINATION WEDDINGS

Georgia Tourism
285 Peachtree Center Avenue
Marquis Two Tower
Suite 1000
Atlanta, GA 30303
Tel: (404) 656-3545
www.georgia.org

Greyfield Inn
Cumberland Island
8 North Second Street
Box 900
Fernandina Beach
FL 32035-0900
Tel: (904) 261-6408
www.greyfieldinn.com

Pink Beach Club
Tucker's Town, Bermuda
c/o Elite Hotels, Inc.
5 Brook Street
Darien, CT 06820
Tel: 1-800-355-6161

FLOWERS

Karina Lemke
Floral Consultant
Posies Flower Shop
590 Markham Street
Toronto, Ontario M6G 2L8
Tel: (416) 588-9061
www.tor.com/littleshop

Constance Spry Flower School
Moor Park House
Moor Park Lane
Farnham, Surrey GU9 8EN
Tel: 01252 734477
www.constancespry.com

INVITATIONS

Lavender Press
28 Gibson Avenue
Toronto, Ontario M5R 1T5
Tel: (416) 998-1790
www.lavenderpress.com

Ellen Weldon Designs
273 Church Street
New York, NY 10013
Tel: (212) 925-4483

JEWELERS

Birks
Corporate Offices
1240 SQ Phillips
Montreal, Quebec H3B 3H4
Tel: (514) 397-2593
www.birks.com

Cartier
653 Fifth Avenue
New York, NY 10022
Tel: 1-800-Cartier

Diamond Information Center
J. Walter Thompson
466 Lexington Avenue
New York, NY 10017
www.adiamondisforever.com

Nathan Levy Designs
42 West 48th Street
Suite 1001
New York, NY 10036
Tel: (212) 354-4363

M.K. Diamonds & Jewelry
631 South Olive Street
Suite 400
Los Angeles, CA 90014
Tel: 1-800-624-2634

Mikimoto
730 Fifth Avenue
New York, NY 10019
Tel: (212) 457-4600

Platinum Guild International
620 Newport Center Drive
Suite 800
Newport Beach, CA 92660
Tel: (949) 760-8279

Tiffany & Co.
727 Fifth Avenue
New York, NY 10022
Tel: (212) 755-8000
www.tiffany.com

Timeless Designs LLC
2 West 47th Street
New York, NY 10036
Tel: (212) 730-1360
www.timelessdesigns.com

Turi
18 East 48th Street
New York, NY 10017
Tel: (212) 355-5005

Verragio
48 West 37th Street
Suite 1005
New York, NY 10036
Tel: 1-800-VERRAGIO
www.verragio.com

MAGAZINES

Coastal Living
2100 Lakeshore Drive
Birmingham, AL 35209
Tel: (205) 877-6000 or
1-800-574-7744

WeddingBells
50 Wellington Street East
Suite 200
Toronto, Ontario M5E 1C8
Tel: (416) 862-8479
www.weddingbells.com

MUSEUMS AND INSTITUTIONS

The Fan Museum
12 Crooms Hill
Greenwich
London SE10 8ER
Tel: 0181 858 7879

John Fitzgerald Kennedy Library
Columbia Point
Boston, MA 02125-3398
Tel: (617) 929-4530

Toni Frissell Collection
The Library of Congress
101 Independence SE
Washington, DC 20540-4730

Museum of the City of New York
1220 Fifth Avenue
New York, NY 10029
Tel: (212) 534-1672

Philadelphia Museum of Art
26th & Benjamin Franklin Pkwy
Philadelphia, PA 19130
Tel: (215) 235-0034

Smithsonian Institution/National Museum of American History
14th Street & Constitution NW
Washington, DC 20560
Tel: (202) 357-3270

MUSIC

Peter Duchin Orchestras Inc.
305 Madison Avenue
New York, NY 10765
Tel: (212) 972-2260
www.peterduchin.com

PHOTO AGENCIES

Archive Photos
530 West 25th Street
New York, NY 10001
Tel: (212) 822-7777

Camera Press Ltd.
21 Queen Elizabeth Street
London SE1 2PD
Tel: 0171 378 1300

Corbis
12959 Coral Tree Place
Los Angeles, CA 90066
Tel: (310) 577-2800

Everett Collection, Inc.
104 West 27th Street
New York, NY 10001
Tel: (212) 255-8610

The Illustrated London News Picture Library
20 Upper Ground
London SE1 9PF
Tel: 0171 805 5585

Liaison Agency
11 East 26th Street
New York, NY 10010
Tel: (212) 779-6300

Magma Photo News
4050 Boulevard Rosemont
Suite 1607
Montreal, Quebec H1X 1M4
Tel: 1-888-334-9270

Magnum Photos, Inc.
151 West 25th Street
New York, NY 10001
Tel: (212) 929-6000

Mary Evans Picture Library
59 Tranquil Vale
London SE3 0BS
Tel: 0181 318 0034

North Wind Picture Archives
165 Federal Street
Alfred, ME 04002
Tel: 1-800-952-0703

Photonica
Amana America Inc.
141 Fifth Avenue
Suite 8 South
New York, NY 10010
Tel: (212) 505-9000

Royal Collection Enterprises
Picture Library
Windsor Castle
Windsor, Berkshire SL4 1NJ
Tel: 01753 868286

Sipa Press
30 West 21st Street
New York, NY 10010
Tel: (212) 463-0150

Sotheby's Picture Library
34–35 New Bond Street
London W1A 2AA
Tel: 0171 293-5383

Syndication International
One Canada Square
Canary Wharf
London E14 5AP
Tel: 0171 293 3700

Time Life Syndication
Time Inc.
Rockefeller Center
New York, NY 10020
Tel: (212) 522-4800

PHOTOGRAPHERS

Bachrach
410 Boylston Street
Boston, MA 02116
Tel: (617) 536-4730

Janet Davis
244 Sheldrake Boulevard
Toronto, Ontario M4P 2B6
Tel: (416) 487-1626

Rob Fiocca
25A Morrow Avenue
Suite 302
Toronto, Ontario M6R 2H9
Tel: (416) 516-0034

Iraida Icaza Photography
50 White Street
Suite 5N
New York, NY 10013
Tel: (212) 966-7933

J. Michael La Fond
342 Keewatin Avenue
Toronto, Ontario M4P 2A5
Tel: (416) 486-6080
www.lafondphoto.com

Michael Kohn Photography
24 Treford Place
Toronto, Ontario M6J 1Z5
Tel: (416) 531-3013

Charles Maraia
236 West 27th Street
Suite 804
New York, NY 10001
Tel: (212) 206-8156

Fred Marcus Photography
245 West 72nd Street
New York, NY 10023
Tel: (212) 873-5588
www.fredmarcus.com

Jenna Muirhead-Gould Photography
274 Havelock Street
Toronto, Ontario M6H 3B9
Tel: (416) 516-0015

David Rappaport
224 West 79th Street
New York, NY 10024
Tel: (212) 724-5668

Denis Reggie
75 Fourteenth Street NE
Suite 2120
Atlanta, GA 30309
Tel: (404) 873-8080

Reportage Photography
1173 Dundas Street East
Suite 232
Toronto, Ontario M4M 3P1
Tel: (416) 461-6617
www.reportagephoto.com

Cheryl Richards
247 Newbury Street
Boston, MA 02116-2412
Tel: (617) 424-7760
www.cherylrichards.com

Shun Sasabuchi
11 Davies Avenue
Toronto, Ontario M4M 2A9
Tel: (416) 461-3161

Tim Saunders
163A Manning Avenue
Toronto, Ontario M6J 2K6
Tel: (416) 603-1611

Priscilla Wannamaker
516 East Paces Road
Atlanta, GA 30305
Tel: (404) 261-1003
www.pwannamaker.com

Wedlock Photography
4160 Main Street
Vancouver, BC V5V 3P7
Tel: (604) 689-5442
www.wedlockphotography.com

Wittmayer Photographers Inc.
347 Carpenter Drive
Atlanta, GA 30328
Tel: (404) 851-9620

WEDDING ATTIRE AND ACCESSORIES

John R. Burbidge
Historical Consultant
12 Stafford Road
Danvers, MA 01923-2539
Tel: (978) 774-3158

Currie-Bonner for Bridesmaids
Atlanta, GA
(404) 633-4395

Fenaroli for Regalia
281 Summer Street
Boston, MA 02210
Tel: (617) 723-3682
www.fenaroli.com

Freeman Formalwear
111 Bermondsey Road
Toronto, Ontario M4A 2T7
Tel: 1-800-665-9333
www.freemanformal.com

Halo & Co
36 High Street
Repton
Derbyshire DE65 6GD
Tel: 44 1283 704305
www.haloandco.com

Romona Keveza Collection
450 Seventh Avenue
New York, NY 10123
Tel: (212) 273-1113

Valencienne
1104 Eglinton Avenue West
Toronto, Ontario M6C 2E2
Tel: (416) 781-6885

PHOTOGRAPHY CREDITS

Copyright © on photography is held as follows:

AFP/CORBIS/Magma: page 99 (bottom right).

Mohamed Al Fayed and the Al Fayed Charitable Foundation: pages 60 (right), 62 (background), 64 (top).

Archive Photos: pages 65, 81, 123 (top left).

Bachrach: page 100, back cover (middle inset).

Baron/Camera Press: pages 10 (far right), 77.

Cecil Beaton/Sotheby's Picture Library: pages 10 (middle right), 59, 61, 62 (inset).

Cile Bellefleur-Burbidge: pages 53, 56 (top and right).

Ian Berry/Magnum Photos: page 146.

Bettmann/CORBIS/Magma: pages 10 (middle left), 11 (middle left), 34 (top/middle left, right/middle inset), 35 (top left/3 inset images, bottom left), 36, 37, 56 (middle), 57 (middle/far left and left), 83, 98 (top right), 99 (top right), 102, 103, 104, 120 (bottom left), 122 (left), 123 (bottom), 125 (top), 136 (top left, middle right, far right), 137 (Elizabeth Taylor)

Birks: page 134 (clock, vase, bookmark, box, and perfume flask).

Birks/Shun Sasabuchi Photographer: pages 16, 18.

Boulat/Liaison Agency: page 120 (top).

John Burbidge, Private Collection: page 39.

Cartier: page 134 (pen).

Coastal Living Magazine (Brit Huckabay/Photographer, Mary Catherine Muir/Stylist): page 162.

Howell Conant/Life Magazine/ Time Inc.: page 119, back cover.

Corbis/Magma: page 34 (bottom left).

Currie-Bonner for Bridesmaids: page 131.

Janet Davis: page 58.

Ellen Denuto/Photonica: Front cover.

Diamond Information Center: page 19 (right).

Eheeler/Sipa Press: page 99 (top left).

Elliott Erwitt/Magnum Photos: pages 34 (inset/bottom right), 121

Everett Collection: pages 11 (middle right), 34 (top/far right), 82, 125 (bottom), 126, 127, 128, 135, 136 (top/far left and middle left, bottom), 137 (all except Elizabeth Taylor), 155, back cover (left inset).

Express Newspapers/ Archive Photos: page 57 (bottom left).

The Fan Museum: pages 31 (bottom), 98 (middle).

Fenaroli for Regalia: pages 30 (inset), 152.

Freeman Formalwear: page 132.

Michael Friedman Publishing Group, Inc. (originally published in Glorious Weddings by Ellie Joos): pages 1, 66, 70, front flap.

Toni Frissell Collection/ The Library of Congress: pages 113, 114, 115.

Gamma Liaison: pages 98 (bottom right), 99 (bottom middle), 140, 141, 144, 147.

Georgia Tourism: pages 158 (middle and bottom), 159.

Bonnie Gordon Cakes/Michael Kohn Photography: page 51.

Greyfield Inn: pages 58 (top), 165.

Halo & Co: page 96 (top).

Hulton-Deutsch Collection/CORBIS/Magma: pages 34 (top/middle right), 98 (bottom middle).

Hulton Getty/Liaison Agency: pages 78, 92, 120 (bottom right), 139.

The Illustrated London News Picture Library: page 64 (bottom).

Imapress/Archive Photos: page 145 (top).

Iraida Icaza Photography: pages 40, 60 (left).

Ian Jones/FSP/Gamma Liaison: page 98 (bottom left).

John Fitzgerald Kennedy Library: pages 105, 111, 134 (umbrella).

J. Michael La Fond for WEDDINGBELLS inc: pages 41 (inset), 71 (top right, bottom left), 112.

Lisa Larsen/Life Magazine/ Time Inc.: pages 11 (far left), 106.

Nathan Levy Designs/Platinum Guild International: page 33.

Lichfield/Camera Press: pages 148–149.

Charles Maraia (invitation courtesy of Ellen Weldon Designs): page 45.

Fred Marcus Photography: endpapers, pages 72, 116, 166–167.

Magnum Photos/Molly Thayer Collection: pages 5, 117.

Mary Evans Picture Library: pages 8 (inset), 12, 19 (left), 46, 89, 138.

Mikimoto: page 41 (bottom).

M.K. Diamonds & Jewelry/Platinum Guild International: page 31 (top).

Tatsuo Motai-Miki/Photonica: pages 8–9.

Jenna Muirhead-Gould Photography: pages 43 (invitation courtesy of Lavender Press), 87.

Museum of the City of New York: pages 34 (top/far left), 38.

National Museum of American History/Ira Hill Collection: page 68.

North Wind Picture Archives: page 14.

Paris Match/Archive Photos: page 123 (top right).

Hy Peskin/Life Magazine/ Time Inc.: page 100.

Philadelphia Museum of Art: page 34 (far right).

Photo B.D.V./CORBIS/Magma: pages 99 (middle left), 122 (inset).

Pink Beach Club: page 164.

Popperfoto/Archive Photos: pages 79, 80, 124.

Denis Reggie: pages 11 (far right), 157, 160, back cover (right inset).

Reportage Photography/ Susanna Gordon: pages 73, 74.

Reportage Photography/Marc Rochette: pages 2–3.

Reportage Photography/Karen Whylie: page 17.

Reuters NewMedia Inc/CORBIS/Magma: page 35 (inset/far right).

Cheryl Richards: page 88.

Romona Keveza Collection/David Rappaport Photographer: pages 21, 23, 24–27, 93, 94–95.

George Ross (originally published in *Glorious Weddings* by Ellie Joos): pages 32, 86, 151.

The Royal Collection © 2000, Her Majesty Queen Elizabeth II/Hayter, Marriage of Queen Victoria: pages 13, 15.

The Royal Collection © 2000, Her Majesty Queen Elizabeth II/Frith, Marriage of Princess Alexandra: page 98 (top left).

The Royal Collection © 2000, Her Majesty Queen Elizabeth II/Winterhalter, Queen Victoria: pages 10 (far left), 30.

Cliff Simon Cakes: page 56 (bottom left).

Sipa Press: page 99 (bottom left).

Monica Stevenson/Tiffany & Co.: pages 35 (bottom right), 134 (picture frame).

Syndication International: pages 142–143, 145 (bottom), 154.

Timeless Designs LLC/Platinum Guild International: page 55.

Turi/Platinum Guild International: page 30 (brooch).

Valencienne/Rob Fiocca Photographer: pages 22, 29, 35 (top right/gown), 71 (bottom right), 96 (bottom).

Valencienne/Tim Saunders Photographer: page 153.

Verragio/Platinum Guild International: page 30 (necklace and earrings).

Priscilla Wannamaker: pages 91 (event decor by Event Design Group), 108.

Gail Watson Custom Cakes: pages 48, 52, 54.

Wedlock Photography: pages 6, 49, 50, 57 (top right, bottom/ far right), 67, 69, 71 (top left), 85, 129, 150.

Wittmayer Photographers Inc. (event planning by Affairs to Remember Caterers, event decor by Event Design Group): pages 57 (bottom/ middle), 110.

SELECTED BIBLIOGRAPHY

Andersen, Christopher. *Jack and Jackie: Portrait of an American Marriage*. New York: William Morrow, 1996.

Andrews, Wayne. *The Vanderbilt Legend*. New York: Harcourt Brace, 1941.

Anthony, Carl Sferrazza. *As We Remember Her*. New York: HarperCollins, 1997.

Arch, Nigel, and Joanna Marschner. *The Royal Wedding Dresses*. London: Sidgwick & Jackson, 1990.

Bain, Geri. *Modern Bride Honeymoons and Weddings Away*. New York: John Wiley & Sons, 1995.

Baker, Margaret. *Wedding Customs and Folklore*. London: David & Charles, 1977.

Baldrige, Letitia. *Letitia Baldrige's Complete Guide to the New Manners for the Nineties*. New York: Rawson Associates, 1990.

Balsan, Consuelo Vanderbilt. *The Glitter and the Gold*. New York: Harper, 1952.

Beaton, Cecil. *The Wandering Years*. Boston: Little Brown, 1961.

Birmingham, Stephen. *Duchess: The Story of Wallis Warfield Windsor*. Boston: Little, Brown, 1981.

Bloch, Michael. *The Duchess of Windsor*. London: Weidenfeld & Nicolson, 1996.

Bradford, Sarah. *Elizabeth*. New York: Farrar, Straus, 1996.

Brough, James. *Princess Alice: A Biography of Alice Roosevelt Longworth.* Boston: Little, Brown, 1975.

Bryan, J., and Charles J.V. Murphy. *The Windsor Story.* London: Granada, 1979.

Charlot, Monica. *Victoria, the Young Queen.* Oxford: Blackwell, 1991.

Charsley, Simon R. *Wedding Cakes and Cultural History.* London: Routledge, 1992.

Coolican, Don. *The Story of the Royal Family.* Toronto: Collins, 1981.

Crawford, Marion. *The Little Princesses.* London: Curtis Publishing Company, 1950.

Donaldson, Frances. *Edward VIII.* London: Weidenfeld & Nicolson, 1974.

Duff, David. *Albert and Victoria.* London: Frederick Muller, 1972.

Edwards, Anne. *The Grimaldis of Monaco.* New York: William Morrow, 1992.

Felsenthal, Carol. *Alice Roosevelt Longworth.* New York: Putnam's, 1988.

Flamini, Roland. *Sovereign: Elizabeth II and the Windsor Dynasty.* New York: Delacorte Press, 1991.

Fowler, Marian. *In a Gilded Cage.* New York: St. Martin's Press, 1993.

Frissell, Toni. *Toni Frissell: Photographs, 1933–1967.* New York: Doubleday, 1994.

Greig, Denise. *Wedding Flowers.* Vancouver: Raincoast Books, 1991.

Harvey, Gail. *The Language of Flowers.* New York: Gramercy Books, 1995.

Holden, Anthony. *Charles: A Biography.* London: Bantam Press, 1998.

———. *Their Royal Highnesses.* London: Weidenfeld & Nicolson, 1981.

Hough, Richard. *Victoria and Albert.* London: Richard Cohen Books, 1996.

Jackson, Stanley. *Inside Monte Carlo.* London: W.H. Allen, 1975.

Lacey, Robert. *Grace.* London: Sidgwick & Jackson, 1994.

———. *Majesty: Elizabeth II and the House of Windsor.* London: Hutchinson, 1977.

Landsdell, Avril. *Wedding Fashions 1860–1980.* Aylesbury: Shire Publications, 1983.

Leigh, Wendy. *Prince Charming: The John F. Kennedy, Jr. Story.* New York: Dutton, 1993.

Levi, Karen, ed. *The Power of Love: Six Centuries of Diamond Betrothal Rings.* London: Diamond Information Center, 1988.

Longford, Elizabeth. *Victoria R.I.* London: Weidenfeld & Nicolson, 1964.

MacColl, Gail, and Carol McD. Wallace. *To Marry an English Lord.* New York: Workman, 1989.

Menkes, Suzy. *The Windsor Style.* London: Grafton, 1987.

Monsarrat, Ann. *And the Bride Wore...: the Story of the White Wedding.* London: Coronet Books, 1975.

Montgomery-Massingberd, Hugh. *Her Majesty the Queen.* London: Collins, 1985.

Morrow, Ann. *Princess.* London: Chapman's, 1991.

Morton, Andrew. *Diana: Her True Story.* London: Michael O'Mara Books, 1992.

Newdick, Jane. *Period Flowers.* London: Charles Letts, 1991.

Parkinson, Judy. *Edward and Sophie: A Royal Wedding.* London: Michael O'Mara Books, 1999.

Probert, Christina. *Brides in Vogue.* New York: Abbeville Press, 1984.

Quine, Judith Balaban. *The Bridesmaids: Grace Kelly, Princess of Monaco, and Six Intimate Friends.* London: Weidenfeld & Nicolson, 1989.

Robyns, Gwen. *Princess Grace.* London: W.H. Allen, 1976.

Ross, Josephine. *Beaton in Vogue.* London: Thames & Hudson, 1986.

St. Aubyn, Giles. *Queen Victoria: A Portrait.* London: Sinclair-Stevenson, 1991.

Spry, Constance. *Flower Decoration.* London: J.M. Dent, 1934.

Stevenson, Pauline. *Edwardian Fashion.* London: Ian Allen, 1980.

Stewart, Arlene Hamilton. *A Bride's Book of Wedding Traditions.* New York: Hearst, 1995.

Teichmann, Howard. *Alice: The Life and Times of Alice Roosevelt Longworth.* Englewood Cliffs, N.J.: Prentice-Hall, 1979.

Warwick, Christopher. *The Royal Brides.* London: Leslie Frewin Publishers, 1975.

Woodham-Smith, Cecil. *Queen Victoria: Her Life and Times.* London: Hamish Hamilton, 1972.

Wulff, Louis. *Queen of To-morrow.* London: Sampson Low, Marston & Co., 1948.

Wydenbruck, Nora (trans.). *Memoirs of a Princess: The Reminiscences of Princess Marie von Thurn und Taxis.* London: Hogarth Press, 1959.

INDEX

DESIGN AND TYPOGRAPHY
Gordon Sibley Design Inc.

EDITORIAL DIRECTOR
Hugh Brewster

TEXT WRITING/EDITING
Laurie Coulter

PROJECT EDITOR
Wanda Nowakowska

EDITORIAL ASSISTANCE
Mireille Majoor, Alison Reid,
Catherine Fraccaro

FOOD CONSULTANT
Dana McCauley

PRODUCTION DIRECTOR
Susan Barrable

PRODUCTION COORDINATOR
Donna Chong

COLOR SEPARATION
Colour Technologies

PRINTING AND BINDING
Sfera International Srl, Milan

LEGENDARY BRIDES
was produced by
Madison Press Books,
which is under the direction of
Albert E. Cummings

WITHDRAWN